The
GOD
of the
MIRACULOUS

The GOD of the MIRACULOUS

Amazing Things Happen When We Believe

SAMUEL McKIBBEN

Pastor, Apostle and Pioneer

WestBow
PRESS
A DIVISION OF THOMAS NELSON

Scripture quotations taken from the New American Standard Bible®,
Copyright © 1960, 1962, 1963, 1968, 1971, 1972, 1973, 1975, 1977,
1995 by The Lockman Foundation. Used by permission." (www.Lockman.org)

Quotations from The Good News Bible, Today's Modern Version,
British Usage Edition. Copyright the New Testament American Bible
Society, New York, 1966,1971, Page | 34th edition 1976.

Quotations from the Westminster Confession are in
the Public Domain F.P. Publications 1981
And printed by John G. Eccles Printers Ltd.

WestBow Press books may be ordered through booksellers or by contacting:

WestBow Press
A Division of Thomas Nelson
1663 Liberty Drive
Bloomington, IN 47403
www.westbowpress.com
1-(866) 928-1240

ISBN: 978-1-4497-9665-5 (sc)
ISBN: 978-1-4908-0082-0 (e)
Library of Congress Control Number: 2013909586

Printed in the United States of America.

WestBow Press rev. date: 07/03/2013

I dedicate this book to my faithful and patient wife who has been an important part of the ministry the Lord called us into some forty-seven years ago. She experienced much loneliness when I spent hours writing and re writing this book. Thank you, Mair.

Most of all I worship God for what He has allowed me to experience to make this book possible and I dedicate it to Him.

CONTENTS

FOREWORD

The Christian life is the most thrilling experience on the planet! Tragically that's not what churches teach today or what most Christians believe. As Samuel McKibben says, "We are living in a day when truth is being eroded and standards are being lowered lest we cause offence."

"The God of the Miraculous" is a powerful counter-blast. In 60 years ministering from Dover to the Shetland Isles and in 15 other countries, Samuel has seen miracles of salvation, healing, deliverance, protection and provision. God's hand preserved his life at birth and has protected him repeatedly on the roads. (He drives 28,000 miles a year in the Scottish Highlands.

This would be a good read just for the miracles. But Samuel is more than a raconteur. He is an apostle whose passion is introducing people to the Holy Spirit and equipping them for service. He has spent decades teaching prospective pastors (me included) in the Apostolic Church of Great Britain and now in Italy. During seven years overseeing my affiliated church in Taunton, Somerset, he opened the eyes of many to the meaning of a personal Pentecost.

There is a wealth of biblical wisdom in this short and readable package; it covers spiritual gifts, prayer, evangelism and financial blessing.

Do you want the supernatural to become natural in your life? If so, this combination of testimony and teaching is invaluable.

Dr Andy Adam, Retired Pastor,
Oakwood Church, Taunton

WHAT PEOPLE ARE SAYING

Samuel McKibben is a man of faith. His warmly written story will stir, challenge and inspire. It may also unsettle us from complacency, or present us with fresh questions about our own walk with God. Whatever you make of the adventure that his life has been, this book will invariably spur all of us to believe that God is the God of our Mondays, as well as our Sundays.

Jeff Lucas, International Speaker,
Broadcaster, Bestselling Author.

Fascinating! Thrilling! Challenging! Inspiring!
This account of the miraculous works of God in our day, should be read by everyone seeking to serve God in whatever capacity.
After reading it, I feel I can dare to believe 'God has no favourites', and what he has done through Samuel, he can do through me.

Warren Jones, Former National Leader
of the Apostolic Church UK

Having been privileged to know and learn from Samuel McKibben for nearly twenty years, I am delighted that much nagging has finally persuaded him to commit to print this glimpse into his remarkable spiritual heritage and experience of God.

Nearing his eightieth year, eye not dimmed nor vigour abated, you will typically find him serving Scottish churches or addressing Italian conferences, selflessly investing in another generation of local, regional and national church leaders.

Men half his age scratch their heads incredulously as he displays an irrepressible energy, vision and faith that can only be described as 'Samuel McKibben'.

This is a book that had to be written and must be read.

Alistair Matheson, Author and
Founder Pastor, Skye Bible Church.

This book will thrill you, excite you and amaze you. My prayer is that, as you read this remarkable story, you will be challenged to live your life for the Gospel and in the power of the Holy Spirit.

MarcusThomas, Pastor,
The Bridge Community Church, Lurgan

This is a lovely narrative of what God can do with one ordinary dedicated person, and it also gives the Biblical reasons why He chooses to do it. Samuel McKibben has been a life-long mentor and a blessing to God's work in Italy, among other places.

Andrew Thomas, Vice-president Apostolic Church, Italy

You will react to Samuel McKibben's book, "The God of The Miraculous", according to your own particular theological stripe. That being said, there can be no denying the fact that the Author knows God in his life, wants to walk with God in humble confidence, and wants others to do the same. For 'full-blooded Cessationists' much of the book will be suspect at best, and perhaps for some, even delusionary at worst. For others, who do not object to being called "Charismatic Calvinists", this is a challenging read that will not only stretch them, but hopefully move them to desire for themselves a closer walk with God.

Samuel's heart is that the Gospel is not just a message to be preached, but a demonstration of God's power to be seen. Many Christians seem afraid of the concept of "being filled with the Spirit", and this is likely because of the excesses which often seem to border on the sensational rather than on the spiritual. As Christians, we must be careful not to dismiss the supernatural work of God because of these excesses. The Author repeatedly argues from Scripture that his personal convictions and experiences are tied to the Word of God.

Whatever verdict readers may pass on this record, the fact remains that here is an account of a man's life and ministry which highlight what God, our Father, can do in our lives when we are willing to be led by the Holy Spirit.

I wish for this story the blessing of the Holy Spirit, who features much in it, so that many more will thirst for God, to experience God beyond the often predictable routine of much church life.

Dr. Malcolm MacInnes, Retired Moderator
of the Associated Presbyterian Church of Scotland

A very simple thought came to mind after reading this book: "God is who He has always been and does what He has always done." May these pages awaken in you what they have awakened in me, namely a desire to see the works of

God in our own day. Having had the opportunity to work with Samuel on various occasions over many years, I know the stories you will read here will be marked with great integrity in their telling. I can assure you they will not be exaggerated to the very slightest degree. As you read, perhaps unbelief will be exposed, but perhaps too these pages will be in your heart the good seed of the Kingdom of God that will bring forth fruit to the glory of the Name of Jesus.

Rev. Kenny. S. Borthwick MA. BD, Church of Scotland, Wester Hailes; Former Chairman of Clan Gathering

Ever wondered what the Acts of the Apostles might look like today? This comes close! And Samuel McKibben is definitely the sort of apostle you would want by your side in a faith challenge!

Arwel Davies, Apostolic Church Scottish Superintendent

PREFACE

"One generation shall praise your works to another . . ."
Psalm 145:4

Because I believe that it is the duty of each generation to pass down the wonderful works of God to the next generation, I have related some of the things that I have seen the Lord do in my lifetime. In doing this I am conscious of two things. Firstly, the gospel is a gospel of love, grace and mercy. Secondly, I am aware that you will have stories of your own that are equally miraculous, or even more so, for which you praise God. This book relates stories from my life and I trust you will enjoy reading them. They demonstrate beyond doubt that our Lord is interested in every part of our living and, if necessary, will do miracles to prove it. He will do this even though he is still in the process of sorting out our lives. We do not have to reach a certain spiritual standard before God will "show up"!

God's Word teaches us that signs and wonders are the God ordained happenings that follow the preaching of the gospel:

> And He said to them, "Go into all the world and preach the gospel to every creature. He who believes and is baptized shall be saved; but he who does not believe will be condemned. And these signs will follow those who believe:

> in My name they will cast out demons; they
> will speak with new tongues; they will take
> up serpents; and if they drink anything deadly,
> it will by no means hurt them; they will lay
> hands on the sick, and they will recover." Mk.
> 16:15-18

The book of Acts tells us that this promise was fulfilled wherever the gospel was being preached. It gives me great concern that we are not seeing as many of these signs today as I believe we should. Is it possible that a whole generation of pastors and preachers, including me, have failed to teach the church to pray and expect these things to happen? Or have we allowed ourselves to think that God's supernatural power was only for the early church and not for our present generation?

If that is the case I find this to be a sad state of affairs, because we learn from Scripture that the Church is. a chosen generation, a royal priesthood, a holy nation, his own special people. 1 Peter 2:9

The Church of Jesus Christ is one generation and not many. These early disciples are not our forefathers, as many would say. They are our brothers. We all have the same Father. God is the progenitor of all believers:

> who were born, not of blood, nor of the will
> of the flesh, nor of the will of man, but of God.
> John 1:13

If the concept of different generations is introduced into the church we open the door for thinking that one generation will have one experience in God and the next generation will have another type of experience. Consider, for example, widely held teaching that when the first apostles died the miraculous works of the Holy Spirit died with them. History itself confirms that this is not true. These experiences of supernatural blessing are for the generation of the whole church age and not just an "introductory offer". Although methods may change, established principles cannot change.

Have we as church leaders in recent times failed to teach the church to pray and expect the miraculous works of the Holy Spirit to happen? The expectation of signs and wonders should be as alive today as it was when the disciples stood at the gate called Beautiful in Acts chapter 3 and healed a man crippled from birth. Christ's gospel and its outcomes are unchanged.

My prayer is that this book will help many in the Church today, including the next generation, to understand what they can expect the Lord to do in and through their lives. I am totally convinced that what you will read here is nothing more than normal Christianity. That is why I have such joy in sharing it with you! Originally my experiences were especially recorded for our thirteen grandchildren to read. I am confident that God will do the same and more for them and all of you who will step out in the service of the Lord.

Samuel McKibben
23rd April 2013

Web Page—Sermons: http://www.thepracticalword.com

ACKNOWLEDGMENTS

It is with sincere thanks and gratitude that I acknowledge the enormous amount of work that my two editors have done to make this book possible.

Firstly I wish to thank Liz Dobson of the Island of Skye for patiently encouraging me at the beginning of this project. From there on she received several audio files from me and wove them into the book laying the basis of this manuscript. Thank you so much, Liz.

From there I wish to thank Pat Thomas of Northern Ireland who has meticulously read, re-read and read again this manuscript, honing it into the shape it now is. Your hours of dedication given to this work have been to me my final inspiration to keep going with this project throughout my busy schedule. Thank you, Pat.

Thank you also, Byron (our second son) for the time you spent in reading the manuscript and making good and important changes. I sincerely appreciate it, Byron.

Above all my praise goes to the Lord who has allowed me to experience the things I've written about and much more. What a wonderful Lord, Saviour and Friend we have in Him!

INTRODUCTION

The snow was falling heavily on the Island of Skye and it was blowing such a gale that it was taking windscreen wipers off parked cars. We were in the heart of a Highland winter. My ministry trip was over and several people in the church proposed that I should stay overnight because of the extreme weather conditions. I was confident it would be far better on the mainland, which was only about forty miles away. The car would get through the blizzard somehow and I would arrive home safely.

I began driving in this dense snow or "white out". Visibility was no more than six feet. Successfully navigating the treacherous roads in Skye, I crossed the bridge to the mainland and came to the foot of the hill at the Five Sisters of Kintail. There I passed a snow plough parked at the side of the road. The driver gave me a very strange look as though to say, "Are you mad?"

The snow was worse on the mainland than it had been on the island. Before starting to climb the steep part of this hill, which rises 800 feet, the car began to slide out of control. I changed down to third gear. There was no improvement. I changed to second gear—still no improvement. The area is extremely remote, with not a house for many miles. I was afraid that I would be stranded there all night. In desperation I shouted out, "Lord, help me!" Instantly the car squared up on the road and drove off as though there were no snow at all. I changed up to third gear and then to fourth and on and up I went. The hill is steep and some three miles long. I reached the top and phoned Mair, my wife, to share the miracle!

What had happened? I don't really know, but I know something miraculous had taken place. It might even be that angels took control of the car that night—who can say? I continued driving through the snow storm for a further fifty miles and arrived home safely. I seldom pass the area without remembering that occasion and thanking the Lord for his intervention.

This was one of my first challenging experiences in our pioneering life in the Highlands of Scotland. Though God does not want us to act presumptuously, He does want us to live by faith. I have come to realize that, if we are committed to serving the Lord, we are obeying one of God's basic commands and that carries some guarantees.

I'm so aware that my experiences in God are very limited, especially when I recall the words of Jesus when he said in John 14:12:

> Truly truly, I say to you, he who believes in me, the works that I do shall he do also; and greater works than these shall he do; because I go to the Father.

I've often thought of Philip in the book of Acts and how he was miraculously transported to meet the Ethiopian Chancellor of the Exchequer. I've prayed and believed for this experience. Not just for the joy of it but because I've been totally exhausted on the return journey from long, distant appointments and my next day was just as busy. On one occasion I momentarily shut my eyes believing that when I opened them I'd be outside my house. It never happened. It emphasised the fact that miracles are God's monopoly. We must always believe for them but understand that he is sovereign.

Scripture challenges us with the continual call to serve God. Jesus himself set the example:

> just as the Son of Man did not come to be served, but to serve, and to give His life a ransom for many. Matthew 20:28

In John's gospel Jesus gives us an assurance that:

> If anyone serves Me, him My Father will honour. John 12:26

We can skim over these words so easily and miss the confidence and security this promise brings. Such words must have been an inspiration for the disciples after Christ ascended and they found themselves in the thick of service.

How would God show his esteem for them? Would he give them a big chariot to drive around in, with servants attending to their every need? That is not what we read in scripture. What we do read is that serving God took them into dangerous, difficult and frightening situations, especially for a group of relatively uneducated young fishermen, but, time and time again, God honoured them by ministering through them in miraculous ways, by intervening to rescue them or by giving them courage to persevere in the face of hardship and persecution. God's promise to honour his servants was not only for the first disciples, but for all who serve the Lord.

It is significant that, after Pentecost, the first way the disciples were honoured and shown to be of great value to God, was by God giving to nervous young men the ability to communicate in front of one of the most formidable courts in the land. This occurred when Peter and John were arrested for healing a lame man at the gate of the temple.

> And it came to pass, on the next day, that their rulers, elders and scribes, as well as Annas the high priest, Caiaphas, John and Alexander, and as many as were of the family of the high priest, were gathered together at Jerusalem. Acts 4:5&6

> Now when they saw the boldness of Peter and John, and perceived that they were uneducated and untrained men, they marvelled. And they realized that they had been with Jesus. Acts 4:13

In front of this court these fishermen eloquently defended their case. Take courage that the promise is for you also to enjoy when you step into areas of service that create a sense of inadequacy.

Acts 5:12-32 provides further encouragement. Here again, when in service, the disciples were accosted by the authorities and thrown into prison, but an angel came and set them free. God honours service and will always turn up to support his servants!

In fact the book of Acts is full of examples of God miraculously fulfilling his promise to honour service. For example, there is the occasion in Acts 16 when Paul and Silas were in prison for serving the Lord. Suddenly the earth shook and the doors of the prison opened. Once again this incident takes place when God's people are engaged in serving him. Such is God's esteem for them that he performs a miracle.

Bypassing many other examples, we find in Acts 27 that God sends an angel with a message to take Paul and his fellow sailors through the shipwreck experience. God's purpose must be fulfilled and he will go to whatever lengths are needed to preserve his servants.

What are we discovering? We are discovering that God keeps his word and will honour anyone who is ready to step out in faith to serve the Lord. That is what this book is really all about. I did not go out expecting God to perform miracles. I just wanted to serve him to the best of my ability. The outcome was that, often in miraculous ways, God fulfilled his promise, stepping in and doing what only he could do.

We understand that God does not always rescue all who are in difficult situations while in his service. Often he chooses to give grace and strength to persevere in the midst of trials. Many have languished in prison, many have had serious accidents, and many have lost their lives. We do not know the complete answer to this matter. God's ways are mysterious, but they are always higher than our ways.

One thing we do see as we view it all is that we cannot expect God to do special things for us when we are living for ourselves, for our own interests and our own comforts.

History shows us that time and again he does step in and do great things for his people who are committed to serving him and this book provides such an account.

CHAPTER 1 ▬▬▬▬▬▬▬▬▬▬▬

Beginnings

I was born into a Christian home on the 23rd of April 1935 and spent my earliest years in Stirling, which is in central Scotland. My father had become a committed Christian in a Railway Mission in Glasgow. My mother was Danish and committed her life to Christ in a small hall in Copenhagen where she attended the first Apostolic Church in that city. Because of her decision to be baptized in water by full immersion she was ostracized by her family. Later she was among the first in Denmark, in the early twentieth century, to be filled with the Holy Spirit. The Pentecostal experience had just arrived there.

At ten months old I contracted double pneumonia. There was little hope that I would recover, but a group of four young men, about seventeen years old, held an all-night prayer meeting. (One was Hugh Mitchell, who later became a well-loved writer of worship songs and respected pastor in the Apostolic Church.) God miraculously answered their prayers.

The doctor said my lungs would be seriously impaired, but, praise God, when he heals he heals completely!

My father had been invited to visit a Church in Glasgow called the Burning Bush. This was held in a hall in Renfrew Street. Andrew Turnbull, the pastor, was a man from Portobello, near Edinburgh, whom God had sent to Glasgow through a prophetic word. Such an experience was quite unusual as directive prophecy was not a common feature in 1915.

At the Burning Bush my father regularly witnessed God performing miracles of healing and deliverance from demonic possession. People were being saved every Sunday—often as many as seven in an evening service. There were queues to get in and the hall, holding some two hundred and fifty people, was often full an hour before the service began. Water baptismal services were held on a regular basis and records show that in a total of five consecutive services there were seventy seven baptisms. As there was no baptismal tank this ceremony was performed in a bath taken from a house.

Teaching and guidance were given regarding the use of the gifts of the Holy Spirit, which were frequently evident. There was a room in the hall where crutches and leg braces, left behind by people who had been healed, were kept. In this church my father was baptized in water and filled with the Holy Spirit. A new day was dawning for Scotland in relation to the Holy Spirit.

When I listened to my father tell these stories there was something that rose deep inside me. If our Saviour and Lord Jesus Christ could demonstrate his power like this in those days, I began to believe that this generation could also experience what our fathers' generation saw. Jesus Christ is the same yesterday and today and forever (Heb. 13:8).

My father followed the command of Scripture that one generation should proclaim God's works to another and so he shared these experiences with me. Because of my father's reports of amazing demonstrations of God's power, I was determined to pursue and find the God of the miraculous. Scripture inspires us to understand that the gospel is not just a message to be preached, but a demonstration of God's power to be seen.

> The former account I made, O Theophilus,
> of all that Jesus began both to do and to teach.
> Acts 1:1

Because the disciples knew no other gospel, this is what they continued to expect. It is no surprise, therefore, that the book of Acts is bursting with stories of the miraculous. This evidence of the Holy Spirit's power, however, was not limited to divine healing but broke through in every aspect of life. Sadly the gospel, to a large extent, seems to have been reduced to just a message to be preached. God bring us back to an expectation of signs and wonders accompanying the preaching of the complete gospel!

When I was about five years old my parents, my older sister, Anna, and I lived in Stirling, where my father was the pastor of the Apostolic Church. I came home from one Sunday night gospel service, eager to give my life to Jesus. I knelt beside my bed and began to cry. My parents heard and came into the room. They knelt beside me and I committed my life to Christ.

We moved from Stirling to Aberdeen in 1940, where we lived for some four years and I attended primary school. Around the years of 1943-44, I can remember my father preaching on the second coming of Christ and speaking of the day that Israel would return to Palestine. This was truly prophetic because it was not till 1948 that this took place. Things like this make a deep impression on a child.

I recall the excitement as we prepared to go out each Sunday evening, weather permitting, to the gospel open-air service at the side of the Music Hall in Union Street. It was a great joy to stand alongside the adults with a sense of pride rising in my heart. There I was, a little boy, standing for Jesus. I can still remember one of the hymns by heart:

> O what a Saviour that He died for me
> From condemnation He has made me free
> He that believeth on the Son saith He
> Hath everlasting life.
>
> Verily, verily I say unto you
> Verily, verily message ever new
> He that believeth on the Son 'tis true
> Hath everlasting life.

Born, I believe, out of those open air services was the beginning of the evangelistic spirit that has prevailed throughout the whole of my ministry. I am so grateful to my parents for the inspiration that they were to me in bringing me up in the ways of God—not that I fully appreciated it at the time. By then I was about eight years old and even then these meetings were special to me, but I had no inkling that in the years to come I was to spend so much of my life involved in evangelism.

Our next move in 1944 was to Dover in Kent where we lived for two and a half years. Little did I realize that many years later I would return, with a family of own, to pastor the same church where my father had been a pastor.

CHAPTER 2 ▬▬▬▬▬▬▬▬▬▬

Formative Years

I was going to become a comedian and take to the stage!

This thought first dawned on me because my life was always full of fun and laughter. Making people laugh and doing fun things came naturally to me and I began to consider that here was a profession for me! As the idea formulated, I wondered how to start—how could I get into the theatre?

In 1947 we had moved from Dover to Glasgow, where my father continued his ministry. It was there one Saturday afternoon, while strolling down Renfield Street, that I came across a man selling second hand books from a big, flat barrow, as was the custom in those days. "Could I find a book about how to become a comedian and how to get into the theatrical world?" I wondered.

I rummaged through the books in the barrow. Amazingly the first book I picked up was entitled 'From Jesting to Christ'. I know I should have bought the book, but I was so shocked that I dropped it and ran off. It was as though God had been standing at that barrow speaking to me through the title of the book. This experience left me in no doubt that being a comedian was not the will of God for my life, and I knew God had better plans for my future.

This did not alter the fact that I was still a very lively young man, full of enthusiasm, vitality and fun. There were many young people in the church and we used to spend wonderful evenings together. It was a very, very happy time in my life and also in the lives of many of those other young people.

Secondary school life was tough and my witness varied from fair to middling. Witnessing is an important part of our Christian life, as we read in Acts 1:8:

> You will receive power when the Holy Spirit has come upon you; and you shall be My witnesses both in Jerusalem, and in all Judea and Samaria, and even to the remotest part of the earth.

Not only is witnessing good for the hearer but it is also good for the person who is doing the witnessing. It produces a spiritual surge of assurance that gives confidence to further obey God.

I cannot claim that this was the best period in my life as far as witnessing is concerned. However, sometime later, when I started my engineering apprenticeship, I decided that I would "nail my colours to the mast." I obtained work in Yarrow's shipyard in Scotstoun, Glasgow. Every dinnertime hundreds of workers congregated outside the gates and, to my surprise, I found that every Friday a group of about twelve Christians stood in a circle with one man playing a concertina while the others sang and preached the gospel to their workmates. The Lord reminded me of my promise and the second Friday I slipped in alongside them. There I stood each Friday for as long as I was employed there and had many opportunities to preach.

Yarrow's, as well as shipbuilding, also installed land boilers in large power stations. At twenty years of age I went to work on one of these sites. There I met men who had lifestyles quite foreign to mine. One ran his own brothel; another had served time for manslaughter.

One day, just before work was over, about twenty to twenty-five men were standing in a circle waiting for the end of the workday "shout." They decided to pick on me, ridiculing my Christian faith. There was a pool of water in the centre of the circle and one man stepped out and looking heavenward shouted, "If there's a God up there, come doon and knock ma bunnet aaf!" To the utter shock of all the men, no sooner had he said it than his cap was floating on the pool of water in the centre of the ring! I have never seen a group disperse so quickly. God stands by us when we are faithful in the responsibility of witnessing!

As a family from 1947 to 1957 we attended the Apostolic Churches in Clydebank and Glasgow where my father was the pastor. I was baptized in water in the Glasgow church and a year or so later many of us went forward there in a New Year Convention to receive the baptism of the Holy Spirit. I had expected that as a "pastor's kid" God would answer my request immediately. To my shock he did not and I began to see what a ridiculous attitude I had. What pride on my part to think that God was on tap! He still had much to do in my life.

After four months of soul-searching and change, I went to the front in our little church in Clydebank one Wednesday evening. There a boilermaker from the John Brown shipyard prayed over my friend Jim Lawrie and me and we were filled with the Holy Spirit. We spoke in other tongues for at least three or four hours. In fact we could speak no English! I escorted Jim home on the bus, as he was still quite incapable, as in Acts 2:13:

> Others were mocking and saying, "They are full of sweet wine."

When the conductress came round for the fares, Jim attempted to buy the tickets but instead, he burst out in tongues! The conductress was totally bewildered and I was embarrassed. Such was the experience that we both had. Each of us was speaking a fluent language that neither of us understood.

I believe this to be the norm when being filled by the Holy Spirit. When I listened to Jim the vocabulary was exquisite. There was no repetition or mumbling, and my own experience was the same. I praise God for that and covet it for every believer. This fluency in another language has never left me. It is a major factor in making the whole Christian experience so real and the enemy is not able to refute it.

Many people ask, "Is the baptism of the Holy Spirit a second blessing or do I receive him when I commit my life to Christ?" The questions that should be asked by every

Christian are, "Am I full of the Holy Spirit now?" and "Am I seeing the outcome of the fullness of the Holy Spirit in my life and service now?" These are the Biblical questions according to the Apostle Paul's teachings.

At the age of seventeen or eighteen years I was starting to do some preaching and had been asked to go to preach in a church in Port Glasgow. I was sitting in the service in this small church and during the time of prayer and worship I had a real urge to speak out in tongues. I knew in my spirit that this time the gift of tongues for interpretation rather than my own prayer language. Having never experienced this before and feeling very nervous, I fought against it. I wanted to be sure that this really was the Holy Spirit and not just my own emotions. The spiritual pressure would not go away, so finally I said inwardly, "Well, Lord, if this is of you, I want you to give me an interpretation of these tongues before I speak them aloud, so that I am sure."

No sooner had I prayed that prayer than the Lord showed me clearly what the interpretation was. Trembling I spoke out the tongue and instantly another member of the congregation gave the interpretation. It was precisely what the Lord had shown me beforehand.

In my growing years, I owed so much to so many who were wonderful Christian examples. My father was one of these. He served as a pastor and superintended a district of seven churches, caring for his invalid, bedridden wife by night and serving the Lord by day.

A short while after my birth my mother had been stricken down with multiple sclerosis. I never knew my mother to be completely healthy. At her best I remember her walking with the aid of a stick, but eventually she became bedridden and remained so for eleven and a half years. Multiple sclerosis is a cruel disease and seeing my mother just lying in excruciating pain, and knowing from others of her exceptional gifting, was a very difficult experience and it left indelible impressions on my mind.

The time when she eventually lost her ability to speak was for me the worst of all. On one occasion I lay on the bed beside her and tried for at least half an hour to understand what she was saying. She just wanted to say "It's nice to see you."

My life was naturally deeply affected by my mother's illness. I especially remember another occasion when, as a family, we fasted and prayed for my mother's healing. My father hired an ambulance and took her to a healing service conducted by a lady called Mrs. Salman from South Africa, whom God was mightily using world-wide in divine healing.

My mother arrived by ambulance and was wheeled in on a trolley. My sister, Anna, and I stayed at home and prayed and as far as we were concerned we knew that mother was coming back miraculously healed. We sat at the window of the house in Yoker in Glasgow with a tremendous sense of expectation and excitement and just waited for a taxi to bring my mother and father home, but eventually, about 10pm, we saw an ambulance draw up instead. I still believed my mother would walk out of the ambulance, but she came out on a stretcher.

It was this disappointment, I am convinced, that helped to form in me, at terrible cost, a balanced view of God's healing ministry. I came to understand that divine healing involves divine sovereignty, and that is far beyond the understanding of the believer.

Through all those years my mother never lost the joy of the Lord. Many, many people who came to visit would say on leaving our home that they had come to encourage my mother but they themselves had gone away so blessed and encouraged in the Lord. She was a person who never lost her happiness, despite the pain, and that was a great inspiration to me.

My sister Anna also was a great example. She sacrificed the prospects of an excellent career to care for mother. I never ever once heard her complain and that too was a very strong example to me. I was going out and enjoying myself with the young people in the church but Anna was at home, accepting that that was her duty to her mother.

Another person who had a great influence on my life was Pastor Hugh Mitchell, who had prayed for my healing when I was a baby. He was the pastor in Glasgow Apostolic Church when I was in my teens. His unconditional consistency set a standard for me that I determined to follow.

In later years, when I became the pastor of the church in Dover, he was our Area Apostle. His profound wisdom had a great effect upon me and gave me an incentive to seek God for the gift of the word of wisdom. In fact it was in his life that I first saw this gift clearly demonstrated. He could take the most difficult situations that we as young pastors would bring to our monthly meetings and he with wisdom would give us the answer time and time again. He also brought such a sense of spirituality into those meetings that we knew we would always leave there blessed and spiritually educated.

It was during those years in Glasgow that I was called as an evangelist and served in the Apostolic Church in Renfrew, which was close by. From Renfrew I was called into eldership and served in a new assembly in Helensburgh. There as elders we prayed for a girl possessed with many demons and saw her delivered. This was my very first experience of watching two senior men being used to bring deliverance to someone. I was so nervous because I was only eighteen years of age and I did not realize the authority a Christian had. The final state of that girl was total liberation from those demonic powers. Not long afterwards she left Britain to go to live in Canada, where she became a youth leader in a big church near Toronto.

This experience was more important to me than I realized, because of what the future held. It gave me the sense that we truly are children of God and the devil is subordinate to us. It was the perfect beginning for a young Christian who had decided to serve the Lord.

CHAPTER 3 ▬▬▬▬▬▬▬▬▬

Marriage and Serving the Lord in Wales

I was twenty-two years old when I moved to South Wales and married Mair Joyce, who came from a village called Penygroes. God has granted me a wonderful wife who not only loves me but loves the Lord. She also possesses a wonderful musical gift. This she gave unreservedly to the service of the Lord, leading congregation after congregation into remarkable heights of worship.

It was in Wales that I left my engineering career and became a miner for five years. Coal mining is very challenging work but the camaraderie is so amazing that only people who have worked in a mine can understand it. Having never been underground in my life, I faced it with serious trepidation. The mine I was allocated to was not a pit. We did not go underground in a cage but down a slant on a "spake", which was a rough train of benches on wheels. On the first morning, in my naivety, I let everyone go first and I was left with half a space on the edge of the bench on wheels that jolted its way down the dark, twenty-five percent slope. No one knows how near I was to falling off!

The language was another problem, for at that time I could not speak any Welsh and "Big Jock", as I became known, was the laughing stock of the old hands because I had never used a shovel seriously in my life!

One night shift, working with a team, we were moving the coalface conveyer belt ready for the morning shift. The foreman said, "Jock, remember this: when I say eat we all eat, when I say work we all work, and when I say run we all run!" That was fine by me. Not very long into the shift I heard him loudly scream, "Run!" Everybody dropped everything and ran for their lives away from the coal face and into the supply road. In moments the roof of the area where we had been working fell in. The wooden pit props, which in fact were substantial tree trunks, had broken like matchsticks. The steel hydraulic posts had folded like paper. All tools were lost and the long conveyer belt was buried never to be retrieved. If anyone had still been there they would certainly have been killed. Thank God that the foreman saw a trickle of dust and knew it was a sign of movement in the roof. God saved our lives that night.

The change from city life to village life was quite difficult for me. I laugh when I think about some of the things that happened. I was a city lad who had no idea how to live in a village. I would walk down the main road and see curtains twitching as people watched all the comings and goings. I remember stopping and waving to them as they were hiding behind curtains. Just normal village life!

Back in the coalmine one day a large piece of coal fell on my foot, breaking one of my toes. Because of this I was off work for a while and of course this provided a topic for village gossip. About this time our washing machine broke down and my mother-in-law told us to bring the washing down to her. Mair put it into a suitcase for me to carry. I can assure you when I walked up the street there was not a single soul in sight. I turned round to wave to Mair, who was standing at the door saying, "Cheerio I'll see you soon" and then I carried on round the corner to my mother-in-law with the case of dirty washing.

The next day I met a man in the village who said, "What are you doing here? I was told you went to Bournemouth yesterday for a fortnight to the residential centre for miners." Someone had been watching me from behind their curtains when I was carrying the case and this was the story that resulted!

The village people were very good gardeners. As a city boy, I had no idea how to keep a garden. One day I went out and bought lots of artificial flowers and stuck them in the ground making our garden look really colourful too. The only problem was it was nearly the end of the summer and I had bought yellow daffodils, not realizing that they were spring flowers! These were some of the enjoyable memories of living in a sleepy little village.

My interest in the things of God was deepening and I was beginning to realize how little I knew of God's Word and his ways. I was attending church regularly and from the outside everything looked good, but I knew there was so much more to know. The Apostolic Church International Bible College was situated in our village. It was difficult for me to think of studying there because I was, and still am, a "hands on" man. Let me get my hands dirty with some practical task and I am happy, but attending a College and studying . . . ? Eventually, with much encouragement from Mair, I plucked up enough courage and enrolled on a course.

The principal of the college at that time was Pastor Ian MacPherson, a man greatly respected for his writing and his outstanding ministry, which in one way helped me, but in another made me much more afraid because I felt so inadequate.

One day, during lectures on the subject of Missiology, we were listening to a tape of the ministry of the late Reverend Duncan Campbell testifying to the events of the 1948-49 Hebridean Revival, in which he was greatly used of God. At the end of his report we quietly waited in God's presence and the Holy Spirit fell upon all of us. Finding ourselves prostrate on the floor we became aware that God was meeting us individually in a supernatural way. Some students were praying, some were worshiping, some were silent. During this time God spoke to me and I will never forget what he said; "There is more than administration." Those were his only words and at the time I did not fully understand it. In the days that lay ahead and during times of resting in His presence it began to dawn on me that I had spent my life serving the church with great enthusiasm and mistaken that for Christianity.

It had been my great joy to plan and organize things for the church. I would plan evangelistic crusades, church outings, and special services. I thought that was what being an active, dynamic Christian was all about. When I was twenty-one I had planned a tent crusade, although I had never even seen a tent crusade in my life. Auchinloch, the village we wanted to go to near Glasgow, had no hall and the only answer was a tent. So I proposed this, the other elders and pastors agreed and I set about organizing bus loads of Christians to support the evangelistic effort in that village.

I remember also organizing day cruises down the Clyde for Christians, and on one occasion I even hired the Waverley Paddle Steamer so we could have a day to ourselves as believers sailing down the Clyde. Doing things like this is what I felt Christianity was all about! Alas I knew little about the Lord!

The voice of God's Spirit was speaking into my heart. God was slowly breaking through my misunderstanding and letting me know that his priority for me was not serving the church, but for me to come to know him and to know his Word. I came to learn that there are far more important things in a Christian's life than administering church activities. Even planning and fulfilling duties attached to our spiritual ministries can easily take our focus away from our personal relationship with God. We must never forget the warning that comes from the latter part of Song of Solomon 1:6:

> They made me caretaker of the vineyards, but I
> have not taken care of my own vineyard.

God wanted me to understand that there was something greater than working for him—it was knowing him! This Bible College experience was a call to me to come to know him. From there on I determined to do so and, by his grace, I have known his blessing in so many ways. Being actively involved in the life of the Church, however important, challenging and enjoyable that may be, is no substitute for coming to know Christ by prayer and studying God's Word in a deep and personal way. To serve out of our own energy is so exhausting, but to serve out of the energy that flows from the deep relationship we are enjoying in Christ is something altogether different.

As a consequence, God began to develop my prayer life. When I was a young man, although I was an elder, I never really understood prayer. One evening, in the Apostolic Church in Llandebie, South Wales, close to the Bible College, we were singing this well-known hymn:

> Sweet hour of prayer sweet hour of prayer
> That calls me from a world of care
> And bids me at the Father's throne
> Make all my wants and wishes known.

I distinctly felt the Holy Spirit say to me, "The writer means sixty minutes", which shook me. The challenge would not go away. I decided that a Tuesday night was the night I would make myself free and to try to have this hour of prayer. I took a clock and went to the bedroom. Placing it in front of me, I knelt beside the bed, ready to give this a try. I prayed for what I thought was ages, then had a little peep at the clock, but alas only ten minutes had passed! The most I managed during that first week was half an hour.

Eventually I was finding that an hour had passed before I knew it and it was not uncommon for me to be there for a whole evening.

During these years in Wales I also began to seek God for the gift of healing. Even though I had not seen my mother healed, I thank God I did not become bitter. There was a longing in my heart that others would not suffer as she did. This drove me to much prayer, calling on God to grant me the privilege of seeing people miraculously healed.

It would be impossible to forget the morning when Mair was at work and I was praying beside the roaring, anthracite coal fire, asking God to grant me this gift. I continually presented the opening words of 1 Cor. 14:1: "Pursue love, yet desire earnestly spiritual gifts," to the Lord and was given a deep assurance that God had heard my prayer and that in the days ahead I would see the evidence of the miraculous.

It was not very long after that that I received an invitation to preach at the Neath Apostolic Convention in South Wales. I was 23 or 24 years old at this time, but God is no respecter of age. The main speaker was Pastor Arthur Lewis, a lecturer from The Bible College of Wales, and a man of God so mighty that I felt out of place on a platform with him. On the Saturday morning the two of us had a call from Garfield Spurdle, the local pastor, to join him and pray for a dying elder.

When we got to the house, we were shocked to see the hearse outside the door and the undertakers already in the house. We went upstairs and saw the elder lying in bed. He was not dead, but lying as if in a coma.

Pastor Spurdle, some other elders, Pastor Lewis and I stood about six feet from the bed in a semi-circle. We prayed silently until Pastor Spurdle asked, "Would someone pray for our brother?" I shall never forget the experience of being lifted off my feet and finding myself at the bedside. I was literally enveloped in light as I prayed for the man's healing. When I stopped, he immediately sat up in bed. He lived for a further twenty-seven years. I imagine the undertakers felt concerned for their livelihood like Demetrius the silversmith in Acts 19:27 when his source of income was threatened by Paul's ministry!

It was in Wales that our first two sons, Stuart and Byron, were born and, when they were still very young, Mair continued to lead the worship in the Penygroes church while I, with our two small boys, travelled to Garnant some miles away, to lead the church there. These two wee boys, who were as busy and mischievous as wee boys can be, sat quietly in the front with me when I led those services in that little church. Both of them are themselves pastors in sizable churches in Scotland today. I'm grateful to say, our youngest son Colin is also a Pastor and leads a successful church in South Wales not far from the church his big brothers sat in.

The 21st October 1966 was a terrible day in the history of South Wales. A very high tip of coal and waste slid down a mountainside into the mining village of Aberfan, near Merthyr Tydfil. It first destroyed a farm cottage in its path, killing all the occupants. At Pantglas Junior School, just below, the children had returned to their classes after singing "All Things Bright and Beautiful" in assembly. It was sunny on the mountain, but foggy in the village, with visibility about fifty yards. The tipping gang up the mountain had seen the slide start, but could not raise the alarm because their telephone cable had been repeatedly stolen. (The Tribunal of Inquiry later established that the disaster happened so quickly that a telephone warning would not have saved lives.) Down in the village, nobody saw anything, but everybody heard the noise. As Gaynor Minett, an eight year-old at the school, remembered four years later:

> "It was a tremendous rumbling sound and all the school went dead. You could hear a pin drop. Everyone just froze in their seats. I just managed to get up and I reached the end of my desk when the sound got louder and nearer, until I could see the black out of the window. I can't remember any more but I woke up to find that a horrible nightmare had just begun in front of my eyes." Gaynor Madgewick, Aberfan: Struggling out of the darkness (Blaengarw: Valley & Vale, 1996, p.23)

The slide engulfed the school and about twenty houses in the village before coming to rest. Then there was total silence. George Williams, who was trapped in the wreckage, remembered that "In that silence you couldn't hear a bird or a child." One hundred and forty four people died in the Aberfan disaster; one hundred and sixteen of them were school children. About half of the children at Pantglas Junior School and five of their teachers were killed.

The Sunday after this we made our way to the Apostolic Church in Garnant, near Ammanford, South Wales. Due to this disaster the atmosphere was solemn and palpable, not only in the congregation but in the whole community, because in that village there was a waste tip that was higher and nearer to the houses and the main road than the one in Aberfan. What were we to do? Were we to turn our meeting into mourning or a memorial service or a prayer meeting for the families that had been bereaved? As a young man I felt well out of my depth. I knew what the people wanted but the Lord clearly spoke into my spirit and said, "You continue as normal and worship me."

We had developed a style of morning service where the whole congregation was participating in worship by corporate singing or individual expressions of worship or prophecy or revelations, according to 1 Corinthians 14:26:

> When you assemble, each one has a psalm, has
> a teaching, has a revelation, has a tongue, has
> an interpretation.

This sacred time of worship was not a time for bringing requests to God. The Holy Spirit began to explain to me that our worship must never be circumstantial or affected by what is happening in the world. There is always some distressing situation happening somewhere, but, be that as it may, God must be continually worshipped. This is exactly how Job reacted even after four messengers of doom and gloom had come and informed him of personal disasters in Job 1:14-19. In verse 20 we read,

> Then Job arose and tore his robe and shaved his
> head, and he fell to the ground and worshipped.

For Job circumstances could not supersede worship. May that always be the same for us! That Sunday we did have a time of prayer for the bereaved, after which we began to worship and experience a remarkable blessing.

CHAPTER 4

Learning to Evangelize

The lessons I had learnt about prayer were to hold me in good stead when I later became part of an evangelistic team. I learnt that, when we were wearying under the pressures of a heavy preaching schedule, the answer was prayer.

At one point the team decided to hold all-night prayer meetings once every month. Those meetings continued regularly for five years without a break. There were great temptations to cancel them at times, when we were tired or there was heavy snow and ice, or when wives were expecting and it was difficult to leave them.

It was through such occasions that I began to appreciate what a wonderful wife I had. For Mair it was always the will of God that came first. We refused to give in to any circumstance and in those meetings we found God at a new level. One evening we felt the presence of God was so near that we were afraid to open our eyes. Such moments in one's life are never erased. They bring a great confidence that God draws near when we pray and that he hears our prayers!

On another occasion we were joined by an elder who prophesied that each of us would come to know separately God's will for the team. He told us that when we met again we would all have the same revelation. The next day this prophetic word was fulfilled to the letter. God had told us each individually to hold services in a village called Pontyberem, near Llanelli. What a God we serve! That crusade was greatly blessed and many people were saved, some of whom are pastors today. This was the beginning of what we had believed for—a revelation of God's will for the team rather than just following an established pattern of holding meetings.

Through this experience I learned for the very first time to hold on to vision. I believe that too often today, as churches and individuals, we are too ready to surrender vision because it does not bring instant success. At God's direction we went to Pontyberem and laid out all the money we had to hire a large miners' hall. We even had a special piano because it was important that the music was good. We were well equipped and we just knew that God was going to bless because this was literally the result of years of prayer.

When we got to the Pontyberem miner's hall on the opening Saturday night, we stepped out onto the big stage and looked out into a hall which could easily seat two hundred people. There were only eight in the congregation! If we had never been disappointed before, we were disappointed then. At the end of the service we began to question whether we had heard from God, but we stood on what we knew that God had said.

Before the end of the nine day crusade there were approximately two hundred attending the services. It would have been so easy on the opening few days to follow our instincts and to have just shut down and given up. To all who are serving the Lord I would like to say, "When God has given you something, stay with it, because He will vindicate the revelation He gives you."

Our experience in Pontyberem led us to hold evangelistic services in many villages throughout South Wales. We experienced a mini-revival in the ensuing days. In one all-night prayer meeting, the Lord spoke through a young girl telling us that the next night we would be short of counselors to lead people to Christ. Sad to say, our faith had difficulty rising to accept the prophecy! It was to our shame, for on the following evening thirteen people came forward to accept Christ and we only had eight counsellors.

During another of these all night prayer meetings in 1963, the Holy Spirit came upon me and I spoke at length in tongues. As soon as I stopped, another person did the same. When that person stopped, another followed. This continued till five or six people had participated. At the end a prophet who was present revealed that we had interceded in tongues for things we knew nothing about, far beyond our individual faith level, but that one day we would see these prayers answered.

It was many years later, in 1982, when I was a pastor in Aberdeen, that Mair and I went to Itabirito in Brazil to open a church for which the Aberdeen churches had provided all the funds. At the opening service I stood beside the mayor of the city and the Lord spoke into my heart and said that what I was looking at, four to five hundred people packed into a beautiful new building, was one of the answers to the prayers prayed in tongues nineteen years previously. What a God we serve! For me that experience reinforced the value and power of praying in tongues.

As a team of evangelists we were very conscious that we were being guided by the Lord to pioneer in the town of Carmarthen. Every Sunday, without a break for two years, we visited hundreds of homes and held open-air services on Sunday evenings. In fact for two full years it never rained between 8pm and 9pm on a Sunday when we were holding our open-air services (some record for Wales!). Many gathered to hear the gospel.

Each Sunday we spent time in prayer before going from door to door. One Sunday during the prayer time, the Lord showed me a specific street in the town. I jumped up, told the evangelists and asked if anyone would come with me. A German Bible student came. We started at the top of the road and knocked door after door, but no one was in. I felt I had imagined it all.

We came to the last house on the left-hand side of the street, which was a big sandstone residence standing in its own grounds. A young man came to the door and invited us in with these words, "Please come in. I've been waiting for you to come. Let me take your coats. Do you want an iced drink?" (In those days we did not even have a fridge!) "Now," he said, "Tell me, do you think Jesus Christ had a fair trial before his death?" We were completely stunned because we had not yet even told him we were Christians and he had no idea why we had come to his house.

Needless to say God had prepared the ground and we had an exceptional time of sharing the gospel. Oh, the wonder of serving the Lord! Nevertheless, I am sad to report that that young man did not accept Christ as his Saviour, although we often saw him hiding behind buildings and in doorways listening to the open air services. It is a great joy to know that sowing seed is never time wasted and the outcome was the establishing of a new church in that farming town of Carmarthen.

At one point the team needed some means of transport, but we had no money. This challenged us as young men to start to believe God for our material needs. We obtained a second hand Morris Cowley van that had carried the business name of its last owner: "Gorseinon Television Service". We had no money to repaint it so, using thinners, we rubbed out the necessary letters to leave "on vision Service." Well, that was true, wasn't it? We did not know how to pay for the van so we got pounds and pounds of potatoes from local farmers and went round the doors selling them to raise funds.

With an undying sense of wonder I remember the occasion when, still living in Penygroes, in February 1966, Mair was downstairs one evening in our rented rooms. I was upstairs studying and during my prayer time the Lord spoke to me. He said that I would receive a call to the full time ministry of the Apostolic Church. It would come from the National Council of the Church that would sit in Bradford, Yorkshire that May. He also said that we would be located in the Dover district of churches. I ran downstairs and told Mair. We spent the rest of the evening talking about what it would be like working for the Lord in Dover.

We told no one. What an experience it was to get a letter in May, three months later, from the apostles at the Church Council asking us to accept a call into the full-time ministry, and indicating that we would be located in Dover. This was the very town where my father had been a Pastor twenty years previously and where Anna, my sister, and I had gone to school. Revelation through apostles is a very real fact! We could have been located anywhere in the world! Truly this was the work of the Holy Spirit. We had not opened our mouths to a single soul.

For me hearing from God in this way was a very significant experience because it came as a confirmation of the beginning of our fulltime ministry. I was coming to the point where I felt more confident in recognizing the voice of the Spirit, something which was so difficult at the beginning because I often doubted and wondered, "Is it me or is it God?"

This is an issue with which many Christians struggle. Are there any guidelines? When advising others on this subject, the first thing I tell them is that the more time we spend in a person's company the easier it is to recognize their voice. The second thing I often say is that if something comes into my heart and I am not sure if it was God or just my own idea, I eject it from my mind and concentrate on something else. If it never comes back then I know for sure it was only one of my ideas. If it does come back again and again, then I begin to accept that this could be a word from the Lord.

So in November 1966 we left for Dover. There we were responsible for the pastoral care of three churches: Dover, Stonehall (later called Lydden and now moved to Whitfield to accommodate growth) and Sheerness on the Island of Sheppey.

CHAPTER 5 ▰▰▰▰▰▰▰▰▰▰

Living and Serving in Dover

Moving to Dover was very hard for Mair. Having been born in her village and having lived there all her life, she shed many tears when she waved goodbye to the villagers as we drove off in our Ford Popular car that we had bought for £25. With us were our three sons, Stuart who was six, Byron who was five and one month old Colin. Olina, our daughter, was born later in Dover.

Being a raw recruit I found the people in Dover to be very gracious. I was concerned about the fact that the congregation there was so small and quite elderly. I could not understand what God was doing. Why was it not growing? We believed God in every conceivable way, yet nothing was changing. And then God spoke into my heart very plainly about the situation saying, "Once upon a time I had a man called Abraham. That is all I had and that is all I wanted at that time. When it was my time I gave him Isaac and increased it to two, and then in the next generation Jacob, and, in my time, Jacob had his twelve sons who eventually fathered a nation." I suddenly realized that even in the growth of churches all God wants us to do is to be faithful and in His time he will prosper the Word.

Much to my surprise the Lord spoke clearly into my heart and told me that I was to give my Friday evenings to the three young people in the Lydden church. He told me to do whatever they wanted to do and not to force them into a church mould. They were secondary school children then, but one of them is now a pastor. Some Fridays we played Monopoly, on others we went swimming. It was a battle for me as naturally I wanted to give them Bible teaching.

The Bible teaches, "Obedience is better than sacrifice" and this was both obedience and sacrifice! Eventually one Friday they said, "Can we study the Bible?" So that is what we began to do. Soon the number grew from three until our living room was full of young people and the hallway also filled up. Then they were sitting on the stairs. It is important for us as God's people, particularly if we are leaders, to listen to what God tells us to do and to do it, even though it is "outside the box." He knows what he is doing!

Eventually young people from many backgrounds came to our home on Friday nights. Over a period of time we noticed one of the group was missing. She was a thirteen year old, street-wise and very tough with it. She had had to fight for survival nearly all her life. When she eventually returned there was a fear about her that we had not seen before. I spoke with her that night and she explained she had been going to another home where she had played with a Ouija board. She had asked the board, "Do you like me?" The pointer on the planchette moved and spelt, "N O." The reply was crucial for her. Because of her background she needed acceptance. She then asked the board, "Why?" Immediately the pointer moved and spelt out "P A S T O R." She quickly shouted out, "But I don't go there anymore." The pointer moved again and spelt out, "Y E S." This shook her badly as she now realized that she was not playing a game but engaged with a demonic power, and she immediately returned to the youth evenings in our home.

For the whole group it had a very sobering effect. As young people it made them conscious that the enemy of their souls was watching their every move. I too recognized that the devil was watching every person coming into our house. The whole incident made us so aware of the reality of the powers of darkness.

A new day then dawned for the churches in Dover and Lydden when we took the enormous step of hiring the Kent County Council Youth Centre called "365" for Christian Youth outreach. This was 1966 and in that Youth Centre there were snooker tables. Snooker tables were anathema to any evangelical church at that time. They were for men who "wasted their lives in riotous living". There were also table-tennis tables and even weightlifting equipment in this "worldly" Centre. Strange as it may seem now, this was a radical move for those days and it was difficult to coax the leadership team, the eldership of the Dover church and my Superintendent Pastor to agree. The Superintendent Apostle also had to be consulted and wisely suggested that we should be given six months. If by then there was no evidence of young people being brought to Christ the project would come to an end.

Within a matter of weeks a young girl from one of the housing estates in Dover was in the middle of a game of table-tennis with Pauline Wade, one of the youth leaders, when suddenly she threw her bat down on to the table and burst out crying and said, "I want to be a Christian like you." It was an amazing confirmation that, if we are willing to think and step outside the box, God will bring people to Christ in the most unexpected places and the most unusual ways.

Within a short time several other young people had committed their lives to the Lord. One Sunday evening a girl, about fourteen years old, came forward and asked Jesus to be her Saviour and her Lord. As she knelt there several sick people were also being prayed for and received healing, something which this girl had never witnessed before. At the time her mother was very ill and had been off work for several weeks. She seemingly grasped the fact that God could heal a person through prayer, so, on returning home, she told her mother that she had become a Christian and then told her about the healings. Contrary to all our preconceived ideas, this young person, only a few hours old as a Christian, prayed for her mother and her mother was healed and back at work the next morning!

From there on, although still leading the Dover Apostolic Church, I moved into a ministry of evangelistic crusading, holding crusades all over the United Kingdom. My partner in this was one of my colleagues, Pastor Gordon Weeks. In one place we were given an unusual gift from one of the local elders—a visit to a sauna, which was a memorable experience for us both!

Whilst on a crusade in Warrington I made an interesting acquisition. The pastor's son, who had been away on an archaeological dig at a Roman site, returned with some seed in a plastic bag. "This is seed that we found in a big vase and it is approximately 2,000 years old, dating back to the Roman occupation," he informed me. He gave me about an egg cupful of the seed which I took home and then enlisted the help of a professional gardener to plant.

Within four to five weeks the gardener came back to me and said, "Here are your seeds." He had put them in a little pot and a very high percentage of those seeds had grown. For me it was one of the most astonishing things I have ever held in my hand—plants grown from seeds that were 2,000 years old. Why had they not grown before? Because without soil, no matter how good the seed is, it will not grow. I have used this illustration many times, because Jesus says that His Word is the seed. Unless our hearts are good soil that perfect seed of His Word can sit there forever and nothing will grow from it.

Throughout our ministry we have been able to say from experience that we have found God is not only interested in the spiritual, the physical and the financial but is ready to provide in every department of life. He is just longing to perform miracles of every shape and size to prosper His work and bring glory to His name.

Here is an example. Because the level of the road outside our church in Lydden had been raised, the whole area that the church sat on had to be raised by more than two metres before we could build the new church. We tried to save as much money as possible, and in a wonderful way we experienced God's miraculous provision and intervention.

We had some rubble to shift so we hired a digger and driver. The driver moved the rubble and then he informed me that he had a free day, so, if I obtained the necessary material, he would stay and fill the enormous hole. I lifted my heart to the Lord and asked him what to do. We had nothing to fill the hole with and it was the full size of the site. I felt guided to go to Dover, six miles away. I believed God to meet the need, although I did not know how. And then, as I drove down to the Folkstone Road, I saw that contractors were moving a large hill of chalk. I asked the foreman if he would dump some of it at Lydden. He agreed and all day big lorries plied backwards and forwards filling our site completely free of charge. Praise the Lord!

Later on, as the building progressed, one day God miraculously preserved my life. After a very windy night and morning, I went up to the site to secure the steel work, which we had just erected. I needed to put steel tiers between the upright arches. We had a pair of unusually high stepladders on site. Standing on the last step, with my six feet of height I could just reach the top of the steel frame. As I did so the wind blew the ladders from under me. I was left hanging from the apex of the framework. I knew I could not last long like that and in desperation I called on God. Within a moment an elderly man came round the corner, retrieved the stepladders and I was back on terra firma. Thank you Lord!

We also needed chairs for the church hall. Reckoning they would cost around £600 (wages then were around £15 per week) our faith was stretched to the limit. One morning I had an impulse to visit Pauline, one of the youth leaders, at her work, although I did not really know why. I arrived at 9am but she was not there, so I walked down to the square in Dover and there, as I turned the corner, I saw a chair, standing about six feet beyond the pavement on a busy road! This is hard to believe, but it is true. It was a well-upholstered chair with chrome legs. There was a café nearby and it was full of similar chairs. I went in and asked the owner if the chair on the road was his. He said he was getting rid of it and all the chairs in the café, so I asked if he would be prepared to give them to our church. Much to my surprise, he said it would be a pleasure, so we were given our chairs free of charge. Praise God!

Such miraculous acts of provision and protection greatly encourage us to expect God to intervene in a wonderful way when we his people are in need. I learned to see each experience not as an end in itself, but rather as a stepping stone that would lead to greater faith and greater expectations. If God has done a miracle for you, do not let that be the last. Praise and thank him and use it as a building block for your faith to enable you to believe for greater things.

By this time I was a proud young father of three boys and a baby daughter, Olina. Looking back, I still had many lessons to learn. I had no problem serving other people in any way and at any time, but learning to receive from others was a different matter. In John 13 we read that the apostle Peter had the same problem when Jesus offered to wash his feet. "Never shall you wash my feet!" (v.8) was his speedy retort.

There was no doubt about it. I, like Peter, had a problem receiving.

In the Sheerness assembly, on the Isle of Sheppey, a retired missionary lady offered me a tape recorder and some finance. Even although we had four children, I point blank refused to take it from her. She immediately told me to sit down, reminding me that she had been a missionary to Liberia, where a church was built in her memory, and that she had also preached her way across Canada twice. She gave me a firm talking to on the need of being willing to receive as well as to give. I realized my problem was pride! Martin Luther says that pride is the root of all sin. How to receive was a lesson I needed to learn.

During the early years in Dover we began to see God move in healing. I was invited to go and preach in an evangelistic crusade in Southampton where, one evening, a lady came forward to ask me to pray for her. She had been married for eight years and the doctor had told her that she would never bear children. At this moment I was really afraid to pray because I did not feel anything "spiritual." I was just plain afraid that this prayer would not work! I prayed a simple prayer that this barren womb would become fruitful. I left for home. What a joy it was to receive a letter nine months later saying that she had given birth to a lovely child! For many years Mair and I received a card from her at Christmas to say thank you to the Lord. Later she had a second and a third baby. God answers prayer.

Over the years I have seen so much evidence of God's healing power that it is difficult to decide what to relate. The incidents that follow were either confirmed by medical experts or were visibly evident as prayers were answered. Many of these events should be recorded as miracles rather than healings.

Twice in Dover we saw God perform miracles. One was on a spinal deformity and the other was on a spinal injury. The first was a young girl with curvature of the spine. She was due to go into the local hospital for investigations. One Sunday evening she came forward for prayer. We prayed, but it seemed to me as though nothing happened, although I did hear later that some members of the congregation heard a kind of clicking noise. Next morning, she had an appointment with a Dr. Thomas at the hospital and when he examined her he said that there was now nothing wrong with her back. It was as straight as his own. No operation was performed. Wonderful Lord!

Another young woman, who was not a Christian, came for healing. She had dislocated some part of her back and was in such pain that the service had to be re-arranged because she could not sit for its full length. Before I preached I called her forward. As we prayed, we saw her back straighten. I had never seen such a dramatic change in any case of healing. She too did not need the surgery which had been planned. This was also the first case where God taught me that even miraculous healing is not necessarily an experience that will bring people to Christ. That person, to my knowledge, never returned to the church or committed her life to Christ.

As experiences like these began to occur more frequently, I found myself deep inside becoming more fearful. On the one hand I was afraid that as a young man I could foolishly become proud. On the other, I was afraid these blessings would all stop and I kept telling myself that I was not nearly holy enough for these things to be happening! On reflection I understand that this was by far the best attitude to have as it taught me total reliance upon the Lord. Well into retirement now, it is a lesson I have never forgotten and an attitude I have sought to maintain.

At this time God also began to build up my faith in the prophetic word. We had two prophets greatly used of God, one in the Dover church and one in Lydden. I did not realize then that there would be occasions when as a family we would stand on prophecy and it would change the direction of our whole life. At this stage I could only cautiously listen and receive the prophetic words.

One Sunday morning in Dover when there were only approximately thirty people in the congregation, the Lord spoke through one of the prophets. He was quite elderly. The Lord said that the day was coming when the place would be filled with people praising and glorifying God! The building could hold approximately ninety people. This prophecy was too much for my faith. I am glad to say that God does not change his mind just because we do not have faith to believe. The fact is that the congregation steadily grew, mostly due to the young people who were being saved. On several occasions in our Christmas services we did not have sufficient seating to accommodate everyone. God's Word says, "Put your trust in His prophets and succeed." 2 Chron. 20:20

After nearly ten years in Dover we received a call from the Apostolic Church Council in 1974 to move to Aberdeen.

Again I was quite amazed that God would give me the privilege of following in my father's footsteps, returning to the city and the church where I had spent my early childhood years. Our children would attend yet again the same schools which I had attended and play in the same streets. In fact the new manse was only round the corner from the one I had lived in as a child thirty-five years earlier.

CHAPTER 6

Aberdeen and Beyond

The will of God is costly in all sorts of ways and impacts the whole family. Moving to Aberdeen was difficult for Mair. It had not been easy going to Dover, far away from the lovely little Welsh village where she had lived all her life, but God gave her grace and it became a place of real joy and satisfaction. But Aberdeen . . . ? She had once met people from Aberdeen and heard how remote it was. There and then she decided that she would never like to be so far away from home, but God tests us in our walk with Him and to Aberdeen we went!

When Mair arrived at the house it seemed so small and she wondered whether a family of six would manage to squeeze into it! How would she fit into the culture? How would the children settle in this country where even the education system was completely different? Uprooting a family from one place to another is never easy.

It is also a hard experience for any pastor to relocate from one church to another. It is only when you move that you begin to realize how much of yourself you invest in a church and when you leave, you leave a portion of yourself behind. Knowing it is the will of God is very helpful, but it does not fill all the holes in your heart. One of the greatest things believers can do is pray for their pastor. By this I mean real, earnest prayer, not just a passing mention. I knew a woman several years ago who committed herself to spend one hour a day in prayer for apostles, then the next day one hour of prayer for prophets, the next day for evangelists, the next for pastors and the fifth day for teachers in the Body of Christ. Your pastor needs your prayers!

It was quite sad to attend our first service in the Aberdeen church. There were only about twenty people there and the building was in a very poor condition. Our children felt it very much as we had left a thriving church in Dover, full of young people. Here there were only two young children. Some of the congregation I had known as a child but now they were thirty years older. Nevertheless we knew without a doubt that God had sent us to this city and it was also a joy to have responsibility for a group of believers in Peterhead, thirty miles away, and a church in Mid Yell, Shetland, more than two hundred miles by sea.

But back to Aberdeen—why should a city centre church with sound beliefs have only about twenty people worshipping in it? There must be a reason—and there was. Some two hundred yards up the road stood a Spiritualist Church and I came to understand in prayer that this was a great hindrance to the progress of our church. Now I realized I was entering a very new area of spiritual service. I began to pray that the

Spiritualist Church would be closed and, within a matter of eight weeks it was. Within a further month or two the building was destroyed by fire. God was beginning to teach me the meaning of spiritual authority. From there on the Aberdeen church began to grow.

On one occasion I received a revelation in relation to the small church in Peterhead for which I also had pastoral responsibility. For four years we travelled there on Sundays and mid-week to minister to a congregation of some ten to twelve people, all of them elderly. Once, when preparing for my Sunday ministry, I felt compelled by revelation to ask God for a sign that He was going to multiply the Peterhead congregation. I still remember the prayer, "Lord, I ask you specifically that one new person will be in the congregation in Peterhead on Sunday morning. I do not care if they never come back again. I ask for this to happen as a sign promising growth."

Arriving at the church at 10.45am the next Sunday, I opened the door and saw in the second last row the back of a man who had never attended the church before. I praised God! We never saw him again, but within two years the congregation had grown to over one hundred people and we had to engage a new pastor to care for the church. Praise the Lord!

At this church in Peterhead there was a woman of God renowned for her godliness and closeness to the Lord. She had a remarkable gift of interpretation of tongues. On several occasions when tongues were given in a service she would interpret, and instead of it being the usual edifying word to the congregation it was a tongue of exhortation and praise and worship along the lines of:

"For thou the Almighty are glorious beyond human understanding. Thy majesty shines above the stars," and on it went exalting God. What an effect it had on the local church with people standing up, glorifying and worshipping God as this tongue was being interpreted, and that happened on more than one occasion. I have never heard anyone else interpret tongues in a way that brought such encouragement and blessing to a congregation.

Many believers today appear dismissive of the gift of tongues. What a blessing they are missing when God's Word frequently encourages their use:

> Therefore, my brethren, desire earnestly to
> prophesy, and do not forbid to speak in tongues.
> 1 Cor. 14:39

To dismiss a gift from God must surely be the ultimate folly. The Apostle Paul, who enjoyed the full advantages of the gift, says:

> I thank God I speak in tongues more than you
> all. 1 Cor. 14:18

By discouraging people to speak in other tongues we are robbing them of blessing. I believe that when we pray in our own language we must pray according to our measure of faith and knowledge. But when speaking to God in tongues, either in prayer or worship, we are taken out of our own limitations and are praying in the power of the Holy Spirit. When we are filled with the Holy Spirit and speaking in tongues we have the remarkable privilege of a "hotline" to heaven:

> For one who speaks in a tongue does not speak to men, but to God: for no—one understands, but in his spirit he speaks mysteries. 1 Corinthians 14:2

This is a gift from God which makes it possible for us to pray beyond our knowledge and our faith because the Holy Spirit is now in control.

The gift of tongues for interpretation, as any other gift, is not given as a badge of spiritual maturity, but in order to bless and build up the Body of Christ. Firstly we must demonstrate our earnest desire to God that we really long for this gift by praying for it continually. Secondly we must ask God for faith to step out and speak the tongues when the Spirit prompts. I believe that, because of a lack of faith and possibly teaching amongst God's people, many churches are not experiencing the fullness of the Holy Spirit. I appeal to you to step out and trust God knowing that, if we prepare our hearts, God will not mock us but will give us ministries from himself that are quite miraculous.

There are occasions when tongues are spoken out in a service and there is no interpretation. This leaves some in the congregation bewildered and it can create a difficult situation for whoever is leading. I have observed on many occasions that after tongues are spoken aloud, even without interpretation, there comes a spiritual release in the service and often later prophecy will flow like a river. Why should we think that we have or must give an explanation of everything the Holy Spirit is doing? He is so much bigger than we are.

Tongues are an amazing ministry. Some years earlier, when I was in Dover, there was a lady who at times would begin to sing in tongues. On one of those occasions it was as though there was a heavenly choir singing with her! Again the whole congregation was lifted up in the presence of God and began to worship and magnify God in liberty.

Paul speaks about singing in the Spirit, and really it is another way of saying singing in unknown tongues. We thank God for this expression of the gift.

So, for the developing of depth in our souls, I would encourage God's people to seek for tongues and to use them in their fullest possible way. God tells us in his Word through the Apostle Paul of his desire for all to speak in tongues:

> Now I wish that you all spoke in tongues, but
> even more that you would prophesy. 1 Cor. 14:5

Our continual prayer was for growth, especially amongst the youth in Aberdeen. Within a few years the Lord had saved a handful of young people and things were changing. The story of one young girl who came forward to accept Jesus as her Saviour is memorable. When I asked her to pray the prayer of confession and commitment her jaw literally locked! Her mouth was wide open and not a noise could come out. This happened at the moment when I asked her to say the two words "Lord Jesus." An incident like this makes one powerfully aware of the reality of the spiritual conflict between Satan and Jesus Christ. He hates Jesus and the Name of Jesus because it reminds him of Calvary and the day of his defeat.

Mair was with me when we were leading this young girl to the Lord. I had never seen anything like it, but understood what was happening. I was afraid that I did not have the spiritual authority to deal with the demon so we prayed over her and asked the girl to go home and meet us again in two days time. She was scared to go home in her condition for she too understood what was happening, and I felt so insufficient for the task.

This was my very first experience of demonic deliverance. As I fasted and prayed for two days, the Lord led me to Psalm 107:16:

> For He has shattered gates of bronze and cut
> bars of iron asunder.

I knew instantly that God had answered my prayers and, if I stepped out in faith, I had nothing to fear.

When we met again I prayed and in Jesus' Name cast out the demonic spirit. What an instant change when the demon left and the young girl began to smile and sing about Jesus. She then prayed so easily and gave her life to the Lord. Today that girl is a mother and has an active and responsible role in her church. To God be the glory!

Here I must share a painful experience I had during our time in Aberdeen. We had a difficult problem facing us in the church and I was becoming weary of its reoccurrence.

I decided that I would take it upon myself to sort this out once and for all. I had decided I would lay down the law. Sadly there was not a lot of Christ-like love and grace in my plan, yet I was determined to go through with it. While praying about the matter the voice of the Holy Spirit spoke into my heart and said "Son remember you are firstly a Christian and secondly a pastor!" That was enough. I broke down and wept repenting of this un-Christ-like attitude and, from there on, the method by which I have tackled difficult situations has changed dramatically. Be aware of spiritual pride!

Other churches in Scotland encouraged and helped us by sending some of their own young people to Aberdeen for our youth weekends, and on one of these occasions something remarkable happened. Although we were a Pentecostal church there was seldom much evidence of power and fire. It was all very staid. That was not an unusual state of affairs for Pentecostal churches in those days. At one of those youth weekends, when I was leading the service, the Lord spoke clearly into my spirit and said, "Call those who wish a new experience in God to come forward." I immediately disregarded the voice, as "coming forward" in the services was not our customary practice, but it spoke again in my spirit saying, "Did you not say in your prayer when opening this service that you wanted Me to have My way and that your programme would not take priority?"

I was now in a real dilemma. In blind faith I stopped the singing and nervously called any who wanted a new experience in God to come forward. To my great astonishment, in seconds there were over twenty young people kneeling at the front weeping. Only heaven will unveil all that happened in that meeting. When we are ready to do what we have never done before when God tells us to, we find he does not fail us. As we take a leap of faith in our service for God, he will honour it every time.

CHAPTER 7

Miraculous Provision and Revelation Giving

The journeys to Shetland to visit the church there were long and very time consuming. I usually travelled overnight by boat, which took eleven hours if the sea was not rough. It could take up to two days if there was a storm. When I returned home one day Mair had a visitor. The lady knew I had been to Shetland and asked whether I had flown or gone by sea. Hearing that the air fares were too expensive for the church to pay, she told me to leave it with her; she had a friend who worked for an air freight company in the oil business. As a result, I was given free air travel to Shetland as often as it was required. The oil companies were happy to pay the bill and my landing charges!

I remember one particular journey. Because there were no oil men going to Shetland that day, the oil company put on a plane just for me. Coming off the plane I walked down the road, turned round and looked back. The plane I had flown in was sitting on the tarmac with other planes and I said to God, "Why do you do this?" I heard the Lord speak into my heart "My son, they all belong to me and you're my child!" I am not ashamed to say that I stood in the middle of the road and wept.

On another occasion I was in the oil company's office about to book a flight and was told that they had purchased a new plane, a luxurious Dash 7. The new policy was that only company employees could fly in it! I returned home saddened but I heard God's voice speak to me, saying, "Phone the General Manager." Rather fearfully I rang him and informed him that, although he did not know me, because of his kindness I had travelled for several years to Shetland at his company's expense, but now, with the arrival of the new plane and new regulations, there was a problem.

The General Manager was an American, and his reply was: "Well, we do not run a benevolent society, but I sure love to help Pentecostal preachers. So go back down to that office and tell them that I say you are to fly any time you wish, and those are my orders." I thanked him and went straight down to the office. He had already called them and they were waiting for me to arrive. Praise the Lord! I travelled many times for several years on that plane.

Once, when making my return journey home, I had a strong desire to visit one of the older members of the congregation who was in the Gilbert Bain Hospital, Lerwick. The problem was, doing this would not allow time for the journey to Sumburgh airport because the one and only bus for that day was about to leave. It was some twenty four miles to the airport. God spoke into my spirit and said, "Can't you trust me?" Being stranded in Lerwick with no bed, no transport and no way back to Mid Yell was not a good prospect.

In childlike faith I said, "Lord I'll trust you." I made the visit and came out of the hospital. The bus had gone, but when I turned around a car had stopped and a voice said, "What are you doing here?" I had only met the driver once before in my life. I told him my situation. He immediately told me to step into the car, then he drove me all the way to Sumburgh in time to catch the plane. What a God we serve!

I thank God for my upbringing and for the example my father left me to follow. Nevertheless there was one area of Christian life that he never referred to. That was the area of giving. Of course, although his wages were low and he had the burden of an invalid wife, he tithed and gave systematically to missionary work, but giving in a free way did not seem to come into the picture. I still had a lot to learn about "revelation giving". Mair and I began to discover that to truly adopt this as a way of life brought us into a completely new experience in God.

One day, returning from Peterhead, I was listening to a tape of a pastor in America whose car had "died." He visited the bank and secured an overdraft. In the evening he went to listen to a missionary speaking. At the end of the service he said to the Lord, "'Oh I wish I could give to that missionary cause but you know, Lord, I've got nothing." The Lord spoke to him and said, "You have got that overdraft agreement." He immediately wrote out a cheque for the full amount of the overdraft! This left me speechless. I had never met anyone who had given their last penny to a missionary appeal, let alone an overdraft. God spoke to me and challenged me to begin to give from a new mind set.

Some time afterwards I listened to a tape by Pastor Jim Graham, from Gold Hill Baptist Church, speaking about giving according to 2 Corinthians chapter 9. He said that God did not just want us to make a "collection" for Him, nor did He just want us to give an "offering", but that we should learn about "revelation giving". We should make this our method of giving to special needs, waiting on God till He gave us a figure. We then must make sure we did not give one penny more or one penny less. Mair and I had never heard of this before. God gave us faith to step into this experience and our lives were changed.

How we long for more Christians to enter into this way of life by taking steps of faith and watching God honouring that faith. It has revolutionized our lives. God points out a need, sometimes big, sometimes small. We wait on God separately to know how much we should give and the Lord always shows us the same amount of money. It is really quite amazing. We still get so excited when the Lord gives us the privilege to be the answer to a need. The blessing is indescribable when we start stepping out in faith and giving in an area that is beyond our normal Christian expectations. The predominant problem is that many Christians live on maximum budget and have never understood what the Apostle Paul says in 2 Corinthians 9:8 (GNB)

> And God is able to give you more than you
> need, so that you will always have all you need
> for yourselves and more than enough for every
> good cause.

By living on maximum budget we have no seed left to sow that would bring us a harvest in order to continue the process of giving.

Revelation giving does not in any way affect a Christian's tithing, which is his giving to the local church where he is a member. That continues unchanged, because a tenth of our income belongs to God. We are only returning to God what belongs to him when we bring our tithe to the Lord and our giving to the Lord's work does not begin until we give beyond the tithe. To the person who thinks he cannot afford to tithe I would say, as has often been said before, "Actually, you cannot afford not to!"

Tithing is not a part of the Mosaic Law and therefore it is still relevant for Christians today. The revelation of tithing came to Abraham four hundred years before there ever was a Mosaic Law or an Old Covenant. Abraham was celebrating a victory over the enemy and the deliverance of his nephew Lot and as he worshipped with Priest Melchizedek he gave him a tithe:

> Blessed be God Most High, Who has delivered
> your enemies into your hand he gave him a
> tenth of all. Gen. 14:20

He then taught his descendents to do the same. It seems that Jacob was slow to learn but eventually, after an encounter with God, he promised:

> of all that You give me I will surely give a tenth
> to You. Gen. 28:22

In Old Testament times the Israelites recognized this long established requirement and practiced tithing.

> Thus all the tithe of the land, of the seed of the land or of the fruit of the tree, is the LORD'S; it is holy to the LORD. Lev. 27:30

Malachi 3:8-11 reaffirms the importance of tithing:

> "Will a man rob God? Yet you are robbing Me! But you say, 'How have we robbed You?' In tithes and offerings. You are cursed with a curse, for you are robbing Me, the whole nation of you! Bring the whole tithe into the storehouse, so that there may be food in My house, and test Me now in this," says the LORD of hosts, "if I will not open for you the windows of heaven and pour out for you a blessing until it overflows. Then I will rebuke the devourer for you."

Have you been wondering where and why all your money seems to disappear? Well, God's word explains it—the devourer eats it up, but tithing breaks his power.

An amazing and miraculous story about tithing came to light some years later in the Highlands of Scotland, where I currently superintend a network of fellowships. A person who had never ever heard about tithing came to one of the fellowships. I shared the principle of tithing with him, but he did not seem to be greatly impressed and never commenced the practice. Financially things went from bad to worse for him until finally he ended up tens of thousands of pounds in debt.

At this time God spoke strongly into his heart reminding him of the biblical principle of tithing and clearly saying that if he would start tithing and stop robbing God, God would solve the problem. All this took place at the beginning of the year and miraculously he had enough faith to believe God and so he wrote out a cheque for a few thousand pounds back-dating the tithes for one year, which substantially added to his debt.

Within seven days of banking the cheque he had a phone call from a man who confirmed his identity and told him he had some important information for him and had been searching for him for a year. There was a cheque due him from the pension fund of a company he had previously worked for and which had now ceased trading. It amounted to over £10,000! This was so amazing the person couldn't believe it. This was the beginning of a series of divine interventions and, by the end of that year he was completely debt free—a wonderful testimony to the faithfulness of God when we tithe.

One day during our time in Aberdeen, while I was in prayer and overseas mission was furthest from my mind, God spoke into my heart and said, "Build me a church in Brazil." God had to challenge me twice by repeating this command before I accepted the challenge. I presented this to the elders and to the churches under my care. I cautiously suggested that we could build a small church costing around £2,000. Wages were low but teaching the people about revelation giving had changed their thinking as well and gradually the plans developed until the church we finally built in Itabirito cost £25,000.

As a family, financially speaking, in Aberdeen times were tough with four growing children. In fact they were now teenagers. Yet again the Lord proved that he was interested in every aspect of our lives. At one point we really needed money for clothes for the boys because they were going to a youth camp. We went to church that particular Sunday morning and nobody from the congregation was missing, but when we returned home there was a small envelope lying on the mat. Inside there was sufficient money for Mair to go out and buy the much-needed jeans. The Lord is our provider.

CHAPTER 8

Spiritual Authority

I had not realized just how many gaps there were in my knowledge of what Christian service should involve. Up to this point I had considered my main duties as a pastor were to visit people who came to the church and preach as best as I could. Oh how gracious God is to allow such spiritually unequipped men to run his church! I had not yet fully grasped the reality and breadth of the spiritual authority that God has given the believer.

Demonic power disrupts families and it is God's desire that families live in peace and harmony, especially Christian families. I came to know a Christian husband and wife who lived in perpetual strife. God miraculously arranged my diary so that I had the opportunity to speak to the wife.

She had told her husband that she did not love him and that she would never bear his children. I spoke to her about the Lord and guided the conversation so that she had to say that Jesus was Lord. As she attempted to do so her jaw locked.

Instantly I turned and called out, "In the Name of Jesus, come out of her!" In moments she was smiling and declaring with ease that Jesus Christ was Lord and I left.

The next morning the husband contacted me and asked, "What have you done to my wife? She told me today that she loved me and also went out and bought me a bunch of flowers." I am happy to say it did not end there. Today they have three lovely boys and the whole family is serving the Lord. Our gospel is a wonderful gospel and our Lord is a wonderful Lord!

I look back to special days of prayer and fasting that we held in the church. Many of the congregation would attend and it was in the middle of one of these days when suddenly a man began to scream. I went to him, realizing that it was not the man that was screaming but demons inside him. I began to pray commanding the demons to leave in Jesus' Name. There was a very great struggle that lasted for quite a long time. The people in the prayer meeting had never witnessed anything like this before, but it certainly strengthened their faith in the Name of Jesus when one by one the demons screamed and fled! During that incident I learned so much about Christ's authority over Satan that stood me in good stead for the many cases that were to follow. Finally that man was completely delivered from many vile demons, some of which had threatened my life. He is still serving the Lord in an effective way and living free from Satan's powers that once held him. Praise God.

At that time travelling thirty miles each way to work and preach in Peterhead seemed quite a journey. This is something I smile about now as, living in the Highlands of Scotland, our journeys are so much longer.

Returning one Sunday night from the evening service I was delayed on the main Peterhead to Aberdeen road due to traffic. This continued to happen week after week and I became annoyed about it. I looked to see what was causing the hold up. To my surprise the problem was that a large house on the right hand side of the road had been converted into a Country Club and people were flocking there. The vehicles in front of me were waiting to cross over to enter the driveway. I am ashamed to say that the delay angered me because I wanted to get home to Mair and the children. How selfish can you be? Sitting waiting in the traffic queue one Sunday night I clearly heard the Lord say, "Curse the place and command it to shrivel up as the fig tree!" To my thinking this was arrogant and ridiculous, but by faith I did just that. Within three months the club was closed. Praise God!

Once again I did not realize that this was God preparing me for a whole new experience in authority over Satan; something that every believer needs to not only know in their head, but to experience. To see the Lordship of Christ in operation transforms our worship life and our prayer life.

On another occasion I went to buy parts for my car from a motor company in Aberdeen and as I went in I saw on the wall of the public area a pornographic calendar. The Holy Spirit clearly told me to speak to the assistant about it. This made me extremely nervous as the shop was full. Nothing I had read in a book could prepare me for a situation like this. It was all about faith. Faith for me is taking one step further than the length of the plank! I knew I was swimming against the current.

I eventually gathered enough confidence to speak to the assistant. He laughed at me, telling me how the customers enjoyed the photographs. I informed him he was breaking the law to have this material displayed in a public place and asked him to take it down. The manager came out from the office and, after much shouting, refused. I left and the Lord clearly told me to curse the place like the fig tree. I remembered this was also what he had told me to do with the Country Club. I did what God told me, and I am ashamed to say I forgot all about it.

A month later I needed more parts for the car. I was holding it together with string and prayer. I went back to the motor company and to my astonishment it was closed. A man who saw me trying the door told me the company had gone bankrupt. Without a doubt, experiences like this changed my thinking patterns, my attitude to prayer and my assurance of the power available to a Christian. A nervous young man, who was so conscious of his faults and failings, gradually understood that God was not waiting till he was perfect before he would use him, but by his grace God honoured his Name even though he was using an imperfect channel.

The next incident involves Mair. There was a pornographic bookshop in Aberdeen and t he Grampian Police had tried to close this shop down but, because of various legal loopholes, they had failed. Mair and I passed it one day and Mair felt constrained to go in and tell the owner that God hated the material he was selling and that he must stop this obscene trade or God would judge him.

When she entered the shop it was full of men laughing and joking. She was so inspired by the mission that, uncharacteristically, she had no regard for their presence or their reaction to her announcement. Sadly there was no change. The owner continued his pornographic trade. However, within three months, while he was attending a political party conference, he dropped dead. A relative inherited the shop and, in a matter of months, the place was burned to the ground. God will always honour those who honour him.

Authority is a promise for all believers, not just for a chosen few. Jesus says,

> Behold, I have given you authority over all the
> power of the enemy. Luke 10:19

Jesus means what he says and intends every believer to walk in the blessing of knowing not just the theory of their faith but the practical reality of it. To do so is a spiritual life changer. Such faith gives confidence to face temptations without surrender and overcome the devil, who has but one mission—to steal, kill and destroy everything we have and have experienced in God.

Colossians 1:13 affirms that God "rescued us from the domain of darkness, and transferred us into the kingdom of His beloved Son". The Greek word for "domain" can also be translated "authority". By His victory at Calvary Jesus took the authority from Satan and gave it to us. This is why Jesus could declare in Luke 10:19:

> I have given you authority over all the power
> of the enemy.

My experiences of spiritual authority were never far from my mind. When walking down a small road in Inverness, there was a bookshop window full of the role-play game called Dungeons and Dragons. The Spirit prompted me to go and ask the manager to change the window dressing. Although she was politely asked she immediately refused. The conversation went on and even when the pressure was increased she continued to refuse. Leaving the shop I asked the Lord what to do. The reply came back as on previous occasions, "Curse the shop and command it to shrivel up as the fig tree." This I did and in a matter of weeks the shop was closed. In fact the whole national company went into receivership within six months. The shop is now a café. God will honour you when you step out in faith

Two of the young women in our Fellowship, inspired by what they heard and were being taught, did the same to a nightclub and in a matter of weeks it was closed. Think of how our communities would change if more Christians realized the authority they have in Christ and were willing to step out in faith at the prompting of the Holy Spirit. Steps of faith are never easy. Doubt and fear arise in our minds. Even those who have previously seen miraculous things happen can experience negative thoughts when they are confronted by a challenge from the Holy Spirit. What is the answer? Believe that God has spoken to you, believe that God will stand by His word and, with that firm belief, step out and believe that God will do it.

In recent years Mair and I have had the joy of attending a small prayer meeting made up of a group of believers that are quite new to moving out in faith in unusual ways. One night I felt the Lord say to me, "Ask them, which is the worst pub in their little town." With one voice they immediately all named the same pub. I told them God was saying that if they cursed it as Jesus cursed the fig tree it would be no more!

To begin with they were very doubtful, but as they were encouraged to believe that God means what he says in his Word, they cursed the pub and commanded it to shrivel up and be no more. We look forward to seeing that declaration fulfilled.

In fact a young Christian present that night was, shortly after this, faced with a demonic power operating in a house he was visiting. On the strength of the "pub experience" he was able to exercise authority and deal with the situation more effectively than many long standing Christians would have done.

This book is not about the writer. It's about the God we serve and about believers entering into their inheritance.

CHAPTER 9 ▰▰▰▰▰▰▰▰▰▰

More Miracles and Encounters

In 1978 during our time in Aberdeen, I was asked to go to South Wales to assist in a gospel crusade in Trecynon, small town in the valleys called. We had already seen a healing miracle not far away in Ebbw Vale, on a previous occasion. A baby had been brought forward covered from his scalp to the soles of his feet in eczema. We prayed for him and the next night the parents brought him back to show us a miracle. There was not a mark left on him except some small cracks behind his knees. We have a wonderful Saviour!

Back at Trecynon, the services went well and several people gave their lives to Christ. On a Saturday evening with three to four hundred present, a lady on crutches came forward asking prayer for her deformed leg. David Matthews, a pastor from Northern Ireland, was with me and stood on one side of the lady. I asked him to remove the crutch on his side and then I removed the one on my side. We held her up with our arms under her arms. I prayed in the name of Jesus and asked her to take a step. We let her go and with difficulty she stepped on to a lower platform. She walked, and then she ran backwards and forwards. What a night it was as God received great glory!

Next day she went to the hospital and handed back her crutches and wheel chair. The hospital staff argued she was only in remission. She replied the Lord had healed her, and left. The following morning there was a knock on her door. A stranger asked to see Mrs. Williams. She said, "I am Mrs. Williams," but he would not believe her. He was the orthopaedic specialist from the hospital and asked if there was any one who could confirm her identity. The next-door neighbour assured the doctor that she was indeed who she said she was. He took out his notes and asked to measure her leg. He stated that in straightening it had grown from eighteen inches to about twenty-one inches, and he did not understand what had happened!

The newspapers got hold of the story and reported it well. It brought great glory to God! In fact when I got back to Aberdeen we found the article was in the Aberdeen paper as well. Seemingly the newspaper in Wales was owned by the same company as the Aberdeen paper!

Of course we do not see the miraculous taking place on every occasion when we pray. Although I have seen some very wonderful miracles it would be wrong to imply that it happens every time. There are reasons for that, not the least that the Bible teaches us that divine sovereignty is very much involved in divine healing and miracles. If you read John

5:1-9 you will find it is all about the healing of the man at the pool of Bethesda. Here Jesus goes into that area by the Sheep Gate in Jerusalem. We learn from John 5:3 that,

> In these (5 porches) lay a multitude of those who were sick, blind, lame and withered.

Jesus, therefore, must have walked past many infirm people before he came to this particular man. Why did he not heal them all? I am convinced the answer is in John 5:30 where Jesus says,

> I can do nothing on my own initiative.

and in John 12: 49-50 where he says:

> For I did not speak on my own initiative, but the Father Himself who has sent me has given me commandment, what to say and what to speak. I speak as the Father has told me.

Jesus did only what the Father gave him permission to do, which explains why, even in scripture, not everyone is healed. Timothy, with his stomach problems, is an example. If anyone should have been healed it was this man as he had the apostle Paul to pray for him, but Paul said in 1Tim. 5:23:

> No longer drink water exclusively, but use a little wine for the sake of your stomach and your frequent ailments.

Sometimes there is also confusion between miracles and healings. On many occasions we are asked to pray for a person for healing but really they are waiting for a miracle. The New Testament offers both. Jesus says in Mark 16:18:

> They will lay hands on the sick, and they will recover.

So when Jesus sent the lepers to go and see the priests they were not healed immediately. Luke 17:14 says,

> as they were going they were cleansed.

We need God's guidance in how to pray for individuals. Too often we find ourselves driven by circumstances in our prayer requests. This leads us to praying for the effects and not the cause. When we are doing this we are only tinkering around the edge of the problem. It is very plain in Scripture that, when we are praying in the Spirit, He will often reveal to us the cause of the problem. Praying specifically for the cause that has been revealed will bring the effects to an end.

On one occasion, when attending a convention I was asked to pray for a lady who was continually suffering with headaches. As she told her story the Spirit was plainly saying to me, "Do not pray for this woman." Then in front of my eyes I saw the word in bold capitals "FINANCE". I told the lady, "I am not going to pray for you, but tell me about your problems."

She started to tell me about her troublesome daughter. I stopped her and said, "That is not the problem." She then started to tell me about her husband and the problems that came with his job. I said, "That is not the problem, but if you don't tell me the problem I'll tell you." Immediately she told me that she owed two hundred pounds to the man at the top of the street and her husband did not know. I then said to her, "I'm still not going to pray for you, but I will now sit with you and work out a financial budget to repay the man." I met her one year later and she told me, from the day she started paying the money back she was free of her headaches.

It was during my time in Aberdeen that the Lord granted me one of the greatest personal spiritual experiences of my life. While in prayer in my study one day I sensed the thought voice saying to me, "Call me Daddy." At first I was shocked and almost appalled. The voice persisted so I was constrained to obey it. On my knees I proceeded to say the phrase. To my utter surprise I could not. All I could say was: "Oh D d d . . ." and there I stopped. I tried at least three times but failed every time. I became desperate and started by speaking very loud, "Oh D . . . ." I then burst into tears and wept and wept and wept. I then shouted, "Oh Daddy!" and from that day I entered into a completely new relationship with the Lord.

Why did I have this problem of not being able to call God "Daddy"? Was it because I imagined that he was always finding fault with me rather than wanting to bless me and give me his approval? Perhaps this is an issue that other Christians face—calling God "Father", but seeing him as distant and austere. This issue for me was deeper than I ever realized and what a moment it was when I broke through that barrier.

From this experience I started to understand that for all these years I had known God mentally as my heavenly Father but now I knew him as my Daddy. Let me hurry to say that I have not lost one iota of respect or reverence for God. My relationship has become so much closer and I see myself as one of his little boys always in need, always making mistakes and all the things that little boys do. Of course Father must correct him but it does not affect his love for his little boy. For me the wonder now is that in these experiences he always responds with love and acceptance, picking me up and setting me on my way again.

I know that this relationship is what God the Father wants everybody to have. You may have a problem with the image of father because of past experiences. Before you reject the thought of this spiritual relationship with God, think of all the things that, in your eyes, would make for a perfect father. Be assured that, whatever you feel a perfect father would be, God is more than that.

In 1983, after some ten years in Aberdeen, we were called to the Apostolic Church in Glasgow. This is the painful experience a pastor and his family dread. Spiritually we had no problem because two years prior to this, a young pastor from Glasgow came to minister in Aberdeen. During his visit he asked me "Samuel, tell me, has God said where your next church will be?" I told him that if he would keep it confidential I would tell him. "The Apostolic Church Glasgow is the next place God will send us," I said. He assured me he never told a soul but that was exactly what happened and in our induction service I gave him permission to tell the congregation what he had been told two years before. I believe incidents like this help a congregation to rest assured that God is in the business and that ministers are not pawns on a chess board.

So spiritually it was reasonably easy but naturally there is nothing harder than leaving a company of people you have learned to love. Many of them were saved, baptized in water and filled with the Holy Spirit when we were there and Mair had many real friends in that church and in the community where we lived. But worst of all we were going to leave Stuart and Byron, our two oldest boys, who had just married two lovely girls, now beloved daughters-in-law. The tears that were shed on the announcement of our going south were many, but the Lord gave the people and us grace to cope.

CHAPTER 10

A City Centre Church in Glasgow

When it comes to cars, I have been told I am a dab-hand at fixing things. However, on one occasion, after doing all I could the exhaust was still not sounding too good. I took the car to a mechanic, a non-believer, who described my handiwork as "being held together with bits of tin and wire". He was afraid that if he touched anything the whole thing would fall apart. I learned since that he claimed "it really was held together by prayer!" and this made such an impact on him that he did not charge for some of the parts because, in his words, this was "God's car!"

When we went to Glasgow our car was more holey than godly; the floor had rusted through! One evening somebody phoned to say that I was not allowed to argue, and I was to go out and buy a new car to assist us in our ministry! I had never had such an overwhelming experience in my life! We had entered a new dimension in Christian living.

> Give, and it will be given to you. They will pour into your lap a good measure-pressed down, shaken together, and running over. Luke 6:38

In my excitement I decided to play a prank on Mair. She had not heard the phone ring, so I went to her and told her that I was fed up and needed to get out of the house or I would scream. She really believed me and quickly put on her coat and we drove off. We travelled to a car showroom where there was a car I had longed to own. "Do you like this one?" I asked and then, taking her over to the salesman, I nonchalantly said, "We'll just have that one over there, please!" Poor Mair was in a terrible state until, outside the showroom, I broke the news!

On the subject of provision we could write another book. This was not the last car God gave us to assist in the ministry. In matters like this especially, where possessions can at times be objects of pride or image boosters, we need to be clearly led by the Lord, who knows when it is time to let go of a faithful car.

An example of this occurred some years later when we were living in Inverness, where I had been driving an old Renault. At times the Lord communicates by a whisper or a thought voice in my head, and one day this voice said, "It is time to let that car go. It is time to let that cargo." We started to look for another one and I began to look at bigger cars, strange as that may seem, because the journeys in the

Highlands were so long and we needed to be comfortable. I could not find anything that gave me peace of mind. One Saturday afternoon Mair said she would like to go into town to get a cake she had been told about. Off we went to the shop but the cakes were sold out, so, with nothing else in particular to do, we drove on past the Mercedes garage and stopped to look around, wondering whether they had any old second hand Mercedes that we could buy.

Mair noticed away in the far corner at the back of everything, perhaps because they were ashamed to park it on the forecourt, an old Saab with a ticket price of two thousand pounds. Enquiring about it, they said they had intended to put it in the car auction, but then decided it was a good, petrol engine car that someone could use. I felt in my heart that God was saying, "Yes, just buy that car," and so I did. That car, which had something like 87,000 miles on the clock, travelled a total of 260,000 miles and never needed any major repairs. The only thing it ever required was to have the alternator rebuilt and it never burned one drop of oil. It was one of the most remarkable material gifts from God that we had ever received. Quite funny to think we went to town to buy a cake and came back with a car!

How we acquired another Saab some years later was another amazing story. Again I heard this whisper from God that it was time to let go of our existing car, which had done many miles. But was it God speaking or just me thinking I needed to change it?

Two days later a lady phoned from hundreds of miles away. This was someone who had not phoned us for many months and has never phoned since but she said, "God has told me you need to buy a new car so I am going to send you a small cheque for five hundred pounds to help you buy it. I know it will not buy the car but it is something towards it." This was amazing confirmation that we had heard from God.

One day I had been down to the Council rubbish dump and on the way back a thought prompted me to, "Drive in past the Saab garage," and there were about a dozen cars on the forecourt. As I drove in a particular car caught my attention, although all Saabs look much the same from the front, and a voice said to me, "That's your car; buy that one." So we bought the car!

It is in miraculous ways that God has proved to us that cars are his and not ours. Within three months of purchase, the clutch collapsed and so did the ignition cassette at the top of the engine, which is very unusual for a Saab. The bill to replace them was over one thousand pounds, but it was all covered under guarantee, proving to us again that it was God's car and I was just the driver. We praise God for His provision and it is a wonderful thing when you can rest in God for these major issues in pastoral life.

My testimony would not be complete without praising God for His divine preservation on the roads, keeping us safe as we have travelled well over 700,000 miles (equivalent to three one-way trips to the moon!) in our twenty-four years in the Highlands of Scotland. Praise the Lord!

Returning to Glasgow twenty-six years after serving God there as a young Christian, we found our church had been given a new building in Cathedral Street, as compensation for the previous building, which Glasgow Corporation, as it then was known, had compulsorily purchased. The congregation had been without their own building for a long time and their numbers had diminished. In our first Sunday morning service there were some sixteen people present and, sadly, no young people. This was a great sorrow to us because our two youngest children, Colin and Olina, had come with us from Aberdeen, where we had left a thriving church. It took some time for them to adjust to the change.

Once again my simple style of pastoral care guided me to do just two things—preach the Word and visit the congregation. I did have one advantage over many pastors; I had a wife who carried a very special anointing in the leading of worship. This had been a source of memorable blessing in the Aberdeen church. There were some people who would have been attracted to the church purely because of the worship. Long before the church leaders came from the prayer room to start the service, the congregation was already worshipping the Lord as Mair led them from the organ. She naturally continued in this ministry in Glasgow and the blessing ensued.

God taught us to understand the power of worship, as we had never known it anywhere else. There is nothing more wonderful than being caught up in the Spirit, in worship. This is when we leave all our asking behind. It is a fact that lives are changed in moments of worship without one request spoken. God is so near, and revelations are received. I also learned at that time, to my great wonder, that in this atmosphere sick bodies could be healed without a hand being laid on them.

A lady from Uddingston, some miles away, was in our church in Glasgow one day. The service had started and we were having a time of worship. The people were giving great glory to God. Some were standing, some were sitting, some were singing and some were weeping. At the end of the worship, Margaret Bruce, a member of the congregation, stood and told us that she had carried something awkwardly at work which had resulted in a back injury. She had come to church in pain. As she stood worshipping the Lord, she felt warmth running through her back and all the pain left. This was something new for me. I had never known such a thing in any service I had conducted. What can one say but "Praise the Lord!"?

On another occasion there was a man with polyps in his nose. As we were worshipping one Sunday morning, the man came to me and said, "I've been healed." No one had touched him; simply the power of the presence of the Lord had done the work. We have so much to learn about the spiritual realms.

Another Sunday during a day of prayer and fasting, over a dozen of us stood in a circle worshipping the Lord. In that circle there was a lady called Mary Bell. She had fallen a day or so before, severely bruising her upper left arm. In fact the arm was a deep blue colour and very swollen. To be able to attend the service that day she had cut the sleeve of her dress so she could wear it and come to church. After the morning service we again returned to an attitude of prayer and worship. My eyes were closed but the person next to me suddenly nudged me and they pointed to Mary's arm. Once again with no one praying for her, or laying on hands, the group were watching the arm return, firstly back to a normal size and then we watched all the bruising disappear and the arm became completely normal again. There was a great rejoicing in the church that day as we witnessed this outstanding miracle.

During our time in Glasgow there were many experiences of demonic deliverance. There was the case of a young man who could not serve the Lord, even though he wanted to. His life from a young age had been heavily involved in the drug scene and there he had become demonized. During the time of prayer several demons left him. Sadly, all of them would not go. I stepped back and called on God for help. Then the Lord showed me how the major demon gained access; maybe we could call it the "parent" demon or the "gang leader". It had entered when he was in secondary school. The Holy Spirit clearly told me to speak to it and name the place where it had entered. The Holy Spirit then told me the exact spot in the school playground. When I spoke this out saying, "I know who you are and where you came from" naming the location, there was a mighty scream and he left. Today the young man is serving the Lord.

I remember a similar case of demonization when the demon was only evident during a church service and never elsewhere. When it came to the worship time the young man would throw down his hymnbook and stand visibly tight-lipped. I spoke to him and arranged a time of prayer. That night will stay in my memory as long as I live. The struggle was fearsome, one of the most difficult experiences I have ever had in this type of ministry, but one by one the demons left till, like the last case, we came to the "parent" demon or "gang leader". Again I prayed and prayed.

The Lord showed me a row of shops and some leather jacketed men. He pointed out the man that had been used by Satan to pass the drugs with the consequence that the evil spirit now possessed the young man. I described the scene to the demons; the young man screamed out, "It was Colin" (the young man actually named the drug pusher I had seen) "and I did not want the drugs," he shouted. There was an unforgettable struggle, the atmosphere in the church turned icy, and in a surge of Holy Spirit power the last demon was cast out. It left the young man like a rag doll. Today that man is in full time ministry. Glory to God!

It is our duty as pastors to teach God's people that on occasions of outstanding happenings and blessings in our lives, we must learn that such incidents should never become spiritual cul-de-sacs but stepping stones that God can use to give us confidence and take us to a further experience in him and in his service.

It is also very important for us as pastors to introduce spiritual ministries into the lives of other responsible people, otherwise they will always just call on their pastors to do the more unusual things. Such experiences help believers to grow quickly and should be seen as normal ministry. In fact Jesus puts demonic deliverance first on the list!

> These signs will accompany those who have
> believed: in My name they will cast out demons,
> they will speak with new tongues. Mk. 16:17

I recall a further incident where a newly converted man came to me and said that his unsaved daughter had a bad spirit in her house and the family could not sleep because of it. He asked me to come and cast it out. I said "No I am not going to do that. You are a believer now—you do it." I told him what to do. He had to make sure that he firstly had a time of prayer for himself and his family before he went to the house. On reaching the house he had to make sure that he prayed in every room, every cupboard. He also had to open up the attic and stand, at least with his head in the attic, and pray. He carefully but rather fearfully followed the instructions. As is sometimes the case, nothing physically happened until he began to pray with his head in the attic. Suddenly, as he spoke the name of Jesus and called on the power of the blood of Christ, a rush of wind came at him from the attic and nearly blew him off the ladder! From that day the family slept well in that house.

I am passionate about seeing believers fully equipped. God has given us power over all the works of the evil one. Make sure you are well "prayed up" and walking close to the Lord, then go and enjoy victory after victory. Never go alone and if you are starting out in this kind of ministry, keep your church leadership informed and take a mature and experienced Christian with you.

This Christian life is so exciting. It is very, very important to give glory and thanks to God for everything, not just for the big experiences like these. Make it a continual practice to praise and thank God for the things many people take for granted in everyday life. Yes, pause and thank Him. He is so gracious to us. In everything give thanks.

As in Aberdeen, the Glasgow Apostolic Church had not really come into the understanding of revelation giving. In fact when we got there the church was very poor financially.

It was clear that some teaching was needed in this area. Once again I began to teach about "revelation giving". This gradually started to become a way of life for the congregation and things changed dramatically.

On one occasion the elders decided that the church should go on a weekend away. We did not want to charge the members directly, so asked them to give by revelation giving. We needed two thousand pounds to cover the cost of the weekend. We received this sum in one offering from twenty-five to thirty people. Remember that this was nearly thirty years ago. The teaching of giving continued and soon the local fund became strong and the church grew in the grace of giving. This enabled us to give hundreds of pounds away every month to various charities.

> Give, and it will be given to you. They will pour into your lap a good measure-pressed down, shaken together, and running over. For by your standard of measure it will be measured to you in return. Luke 6:38

Furthermore we saw sums of over £15,000 and £20,000 given to the missionary collections at two New Year Conventions. Again that was a huge amount of money in those days.

I had not forgotten the unique experiences that we had had in Aberdeen in relation to spiritual authority, but it never seemed to come into the frame in Glasgow till one day I was passing a very disreputable pub. I saw an attendant pushing a young lady out of the premises and she stumbled down the steps to the pavement. It was abhorrent and my spirit was deeply angered. Sensing God speaking to me the Spirit said, "Stop and curse the place." I did. It was a Friday afternoon and on the Monday it was in the evening paper that the owner had been kidnapped—yes kidnapped! Within a month or two the premises were closed and never opened again as a pub. God moves in mysterious ways! Believers have authority and all God encourages us to do is listen to his voice and obey it. He does the rest.

Prophetic words of knowledge are very wonderful. They are so essential for those who receive them as they act like sign posts in their lives. A young man was pointed out to me by the Holy Spirit in a service one day. The word I received from the Holy Spirit, which I gave him in the service, was that in the future he would care for the field and his wife would care for the young plants. This happened in a church many miles away from our home with which I had no contact. About four or five years later the man came to me. He was now a pastor—caring for the field—and his wife was the youth leader—caring for the plants—in a district of churches. He assured me that the prophetic word they received that night changed their whole mindset and redirected their way of living, because they then knew that God had something very special for them to do for Him.

This word was not given to them privately because I had called one of the local church leaders to be with me to judge and weigh it. Personal words that are given outside a church setting can be very dangerous and very damaging. I have known lives seriously affected, and sometimes destroyed, by maverick prophets or visionaries. 1 Corinthians 14 makes it clear that gifts are for the church and not for private use.

The gifts of the Holy Spirit should operate under the covering of local church leadership and whenever possible a church leader should be present before a prophetic word or word of knowledge is given. I have observed that this seems to bring an end to strange and mystical types of personal prophecies and "pictures" which can cause untold damage. There are many Christians who are totally baffled by unfulfilled "words" but are too embarrassed to talk about them in case they get the blame for their being unfulfilled.

I am continually grateful to God for the problems that arose in the early church in Corinth otherwise we would not have had the firm guidance that makes it possible to manage such powerful gifts in the church today. One of the early Apostolic Church pastors made quite a profound statement on this subject: "Pentecost without government is like Samson without eyes."

On one occasion a young lady came out for prayer and asked for counsel. She was courting an unsaved boy and he wanted to marry her. I knew nothing of this. The Lord spoke and said, "Break this relationship with this man for this is not my will for your life. I have a husband for you who will love me and you will serve me together for My glory." I was deeply concerned when I gave this word and she assured me she would break the relationship with him.

Years went by and she continued to faithfully serve the Lord, believing the word would come to pass. I was asked to make a diversion to my journey one day and my colleague and I were invited to stay in a home. We arrived, a lady opened the door with her husband standing by, and it was the same woman. She had prayed and believed and waited for thirteen years. Six months before the day we arrived God honored her faithfulness and she married a fine Christian. What a thrill it was for me to see them both standing at the door to welcome us into their home. Hallelujah!

But are words of knowledge only for church settings? Is God interested in a man's business, for example? To my surprise I found out that he is. When away from home on another occasion, I came to the breakfast table and my host, a pastor in the local church said, "My cousin has a business that is going downhill, will you come and pray that it will prosper."!

I had never been challenged like this in my life before and I was nervous. We went to the business, and it was very clear it was in bad shape because the Industrial Unit where it was based was almost empty. The owner was a faithful and generous Christian. We had a time of prayer with him and all the staff. When praying I felt the Lord said to me, "You are looking at Gideon's army." I told them this and we left the premises.

Early the next morning the Lord woke me and said, "I gave Gideon ONE idea." "Yes", I thought, "that was true—the pitcher with a flame and a trumpet." While I was having breakfast the pastor returned from visiting his cousin. When he said, "My cousin has had an idea but he does not know if it is from God or just his idea", I told him with great excitement about the strong thought that had come to me whilst in bed. The end result was that the cousin implemented the idea and the business is back in profit—Glory to God!

There are other occasions when the timing of the delivery of the prophetic word is all important. It requires obedience to the prompting of the Holy Spirit. An illustration of this was when I received a word for a church member telling her not to sell her flat. It made no sense, so I thought it was maybe for some time in the future. I carried this word for about ten days until, during the Sunday meeting, the Lord told me that I must tell her that day or it would be too late. On the way out of the church I hesitantly said to her that she was not to sell her flat. I was totally amazed when I saw her mouth gape open as, unbeknown to me, that very morning she had asked the Lord for a word of encouragement as the plans for selling her flat were not going well and she had felt a kind of darkness over her. She acted on the word of knowledge, cancelling all her plans. The darkness left and peace returned.

After four years living in Glasgow I attended our church's annual National Council where decisions were made regarding the relocation of pastors. Whilst living in Aberdeen we had had the privilege of starting a church in Inverness over one hundred miles away. It was tough going but the Lord blessed and something was deposited in our hearts for the Highlands of Scotland. When we had been appointed to Glasgow, the Highlands really never left our minds.

The Apostolic Church government operates through the five-fold ministries of Ephesians 4:11:

> And He gave some as apostles, and some as prophets, and some as evangelists and some as pastors and teachers.

It has been the norm, since the restoration of this revelation at the turn of the twentieth century, for the church council to recognize and call men to each of these ministries—a practice which is now widespread in many parts of the Body of Christ. It was within this context that our own move to the Highlands came about.

At this Council in 1987, the Lord spoke through one of the recognized prophets, saying that it was the time for the church to invest in the Highlands of Scotland and that he was sending Pastor McKibben and his family to Inverness to pioneer the work. It was an awesome moment in my life and I dropped to the floor weeping. I did not hear the rest of the prophecy but later received a transcript which said that, at the call, I would weep and not be able to be comforted, which is exactly what happened as the word was being given.

I took it for granted that by the autumn of that year we would have left the city centre church in Glasgow and be settled in Inverness. However, it is the responsibility of the apostles who make up the church Council to consider and judge all directive prophecy, and this they did with the prophecy regarding our move to the Highlands. Their conclusion was that it truly was a word from the Lord, but that it was premature. They felt the move should be postponed for eighteen months to allow me to conclude my ministry in the Glasgow church and then head for Inverness. Their decision was an accurate one, because we were later to understand that if we had gone to the Highlands earlier, the ground would not have been fully prepared spiritually for our coming.

When we arrived eighteen months later everything just fitted into place and we watched God do miracle after miracle, both in practical and spiritual matters. This to me endorses the text:

> And God has appointed in the church, first apostles. 1 Cor. 12:28

It is God's design that the church be led not by one man's prophetic revelations but by a group of apostles who, in the cold light of day, can spiritually judge the words which have been delivered and discern the will of God.

CHAPTER 11 ▰▰▰▰▰▰▰

Pioneering in the Highlands of Scotland

How could it be? Yet another phone call from people I thought would be so ready to participate. It was disappointing— unbelievable even, because to me evangelism is the heart of the gospel message. Within weeks of coming to the Highlands of Scotland I had been asked by the Billy Graham Association to arrange satellite crusades that would be linked to the Scottish Central Belt Crusade which Billy Graham was to hold. I was also to train the people in preparation for counselling and ministry.

All I thought I needed to do was to create a list of ministers' phone numbers, tell them about the proposed project and ask if they would be willing to be involved on a committee to organize this with me. Each minister, one after another, said, "Who are you? What church are you attached to?" When I told them that I was the pastor of a Pentecostal church, each one replied, "Oh no, no, I'm not interested in that thank you." I contacted about a dozen ministers in Inverness and got the same response. I was absolutely heartbroken and simply asked the Lord what I should do.

Because what happened next was such an awesome experience, I remember the exact spot where I was standing and weeping when the Lord spoke to me. He spoke very plainly in a strong thought voice, "Proceed, you, me and the telephone directory and we'll do it together." I just said, "OK Lord, we'll do it together." I took the phone book and searched for names of ministers throughout the Highlands. Eventually, by God's grace, we set up many different centres for satellite services and it was a very, very fruitful time.

I also had the privilege of teaching the Billy Graham Christian Life and Witness course in various locations such as Dingwall, Culloden, Wick, Lybster, Inverness and Gairloch. God mightily blessed in each place. Through these courses, by his grace and his divine wisdom, we were introduced to the Highlands and we thank God for the many friendships that formed and the many people that were saved through the training and satellite services.

Whenever Christians serve the Lord by working together openheartedly with believers from other groups and church backgrounds God invariably blesses. In the words of the psalmist,

> Behold, how good and how pleasant it is for brothers to dwell together in unity! It is like the precious oil upon the head, coming down upon the beard, even Aaron's beard, coming down

> upon the edge of his robes. It is like the dew
> of Hermon coming down upon the mountains
> of Zion; for there the LORD commanded the
> blessing-life forever. Ps.133

To my knowledge, it is the only scripture and situation in which God says he will command a blessing. Unity between believers is God's heart and he endorses it by this promise of blessing. This whole project was a wonderful time in our lives and we praise God for it.

In all our years in ministry we had never before been located in a place where there was no building and no established congregation. The Glasgow area churches had sent us off with a farewell service and with their blessing. Colin, our youngest son, remained in Glasgow, but our daughter, Olina, moved with us, and so we arrived in Inverness. Sitting down on the settee we looked at each other and said, "Welcome— but what do we do now?"

It felt strange, but we laughed and Mair and I decided to put a small advert in the paper to say that on Sunday mornings in Bethel, which was the name we had given our new home, there would be worship, a time of Bible study and communion. Each Sunday morning we sat, together with two friends we had known from previous days in Inverness, and waited—but not for long. Miraculously the work grew. Even though our lounge and dining room combined could hold twenty-five people, we soon had to look for a hall.

There were several occasions when we received exceptional prophetic statements regarding growth. Before we had started the services in the house, and even before we were properly unpacked, Mair had noticed an advert for the Full Gospel Businessman's Fellowship International at a nearby hotel. Despite my reluctance, we attended, because Mair felt that we should go. There were about one hundred people there, which surprised us, because it was a considerable number for the Highlands. The leader introduced the several ministers that were present in the meeting, including myself.

After a time of worship, the speaker from Ayrshire said he had a word from the Lord for one of the ministers present— for Pastor Samuel McKibben. Mair and I were stunned as I was unknown to them in that area.

> Enlarge the place of your tent," he said. "Stretch out the curtains of your dwellings, spare not; lengthen your cords and strengthen your pegs. For you will spread abroad to the right and to the left. And your descendants will possess nations and will resettle the desolate cities. Fear not, for you will not be put to shame; and do not feel humiliated, for you will not be disgraced; but you will forget the shame of your youth, and the reproach of your widowhood you will remember no more. For your husband is your Maker, whose name is the LORD of hosts; and your Redeemer is the Holy One of Israel, who is called the God of all the earth. For the LORD has called you, like a wife forsaken and grieved in spirit, even like a wife of one's youth when she is rejected, says your God. Isa. 54:2-6

God was going to expand our borders and bless us! Strangely, that very afternoon, we had gone into a furniture store where we had seen nine plastic chairs, which I had felt prompted to buy for a bargain price of two pounds each. God was already leading us in line with this prophecy!

We were continually being faced by the consequences of extreme Calvinism, which is adhered to by many in the Highlands of Scotland. Often people to whom we spoke would say, "Don't bother about me because I'm the black sheep of the family. There's no chance of me becoming a Christian." I did not understand this initially until I read the Westminster Confession of Faith, which is the statement of doctrine for Calvinist theology. I then came to realize it teaches that God has predestined some to go to heaven by His grace and others, by his divine wisdom, to go to hell.

This is the actual wording:

III. By the decree of God, for the manifestation of His glory, some men and angels are predestined into everlasting life, and others foreordained to everlasting death.

IV. These angels and men thus predestined and foreordained are particularly and unchangeably designed and their number is so certain and definite that it cannot be either increased or diminished.

V. Those of mankind that are predestined unto life, God, before the foundation of the world was laid, according to His eternal and immutable purpose, and the secret counsel and good pleasure of His will, hath chosen in Christ unto everlasting glory, out of His mere free grace and love, without any foresight or faith or good works, or perseverance in either of them, or any other thing in the creature,

has conditions, or causes moving Him thereunto;
and all to the praise of His glorious grace.

VI. As God hath appointed the elect unto glory, so hath
He, by the eternal and most free purpose of His will,
foreordained all the means thereunto. Whereby
they who are elected being fallen in Adam, are
redeemed by Christ; are effectively called unto
faith in Christ by His Spirit working in due season;
are justified, adopted, sanctified, and kept by His
power through faith unto salvation. Neither are
any other redeemed by Christ, effectually called,
justified, adopted, sanctified, and saved but the
elect only.

VII. The rest of mankind, God was pleased, unto the
unsearchable counsel of His own will, whereby He
extendeth or withholdeth mercy as He pleaseth, for
the glory of His sovereign power over His creatures,
to pass by, and to ordain them to dishonor and
wrath for their sin, to the praise of His glorious
justice.' (Free Presbyterian Publication ISBN
0902506080)

This is a heavy doctrine indeed. The effects are far-reaching
in the Highlands. I recall the occasion when one young
girl came to see us in a state of brokenness. She had been
wonderfully saved, filled with the Holy Spirit, speaking in
tongues and had become truly blessed of God in her life
as well as being a blessing to many others. She went back
home to the Isle of Lewis to see her family. On returning
she asked to see us. When Mair and I met with her, her first
words were, "I've come to tell you that I am not saved. I
will have to leave the Fellowship because I am not saved and
I just have to accept that. I've been speaking to my mother

who said not to believe what I have been told in Inverness because the fact of the matter is I am not saved and I never can be saved. God has not chosen me to go to heaven."

"But that can't be true," I replied, "because you are saved and you have been baptized in water and filled by the Holy Spirit and you are a very effective Christian in the community." When she denied this I asked her to explain. These were her words, "When my mother was carrying my brothers they both leapt in her womb and she knew that they were the elect of God, but when she was carrying me I did not leap in her womb, so she knew then that I was destined to hell and therefore I can never be a Christian."

I sat there absolutely shocked, praying, "Lord, help me. What do I say to this girl?" Suddenly the Lord spoke to me and took me in my mind to 1 Samuel 16: 1-12, where Jesse is visited by Samuel the prophet. When Samuel tells him he wants to see his sons and anoint one as king, Jesse chose the children that he thought were eligible and presented them to Samuel one at a time. Each one that Jesse chose God rejected until Samuel said, "Have you no more?" Jesse finally mentioned David. "Well there's a boy out in the field looking after the sheep." As soon as David appeared Samuel said, "This is God's choice."

So I said to this girl, who was broken hearted thinking she could never be a Christian because she was not elected, "Your mother can make her choice, but the final say is with God." I reminded her of the story of Samuel's visit to Jesse's house and how the one Jesse rejected was the very one that God had chosen to be king. I reassured her that, whatever may happen or may not happen to her brothers, and even though her mother considered her rejected by God, in actual fact God had wonderfully saved her. In ways like this we continued to deal with the legacy of extreme Calvinism. Soon our house was too small, and then the first hall we rented became too small. In that hall we had seen great things happen. None of the congregation will forget the night of divine healings and miracles in November 1989. I was teaching the church about the gifts of the Holy Spirit and on this night the subject was the gift of miracles. Before the meeting I had a witness in my heart that I would not need to preach on miracles—God was going to perform some that night!

We started with worship, and then I called the people to indicate if they wanted prayer. One person who asked to be prayed for was Betty Robertson, who had Crohn's disease, a digestive disorder. Due to her illness her weight had dropped to around seven stone. As we prayed she shook from head to foot. The disease, which is only rarely completely curable with surgery and strong drugs, left her. She still keeps the unused prescription for her allocation of drugs as a memento. It is dated 9th November 1989. What a miracle!

Another case was that of a young girl who had had a serious accident in her work place, severing a tendon and leaving her unable to flex one finger. She was pursuing, and had almost completed, a legal claim that would have given her good compensation. We prayed for her finger and instantly the finger bent normally. Isn't God wonderful? The legal case was dropped.

At another meeting a young girl came forward for prayer because of frequent headaches. The Lord clearly told me not to pray for healing. I told her so, and asked what the real problem was. The Lord had placed before me the word "relationship." She made small talk about several things, but I replied these were not the issues. Eventually she told me that she was courting an unsaved boy and her family did not know. I advised her to break it off and she would be well. She later testified that she never had another headache from the day she ended the relationship.

Witnessing for Christ has remained an important part of my Christian life. It is not only an exciting experience, it can also be a very rewarding one, especially when we take the plunge and share Christ in unusual circumstances, as the following incident, illustrates.

I was away from Inverness and wanted to buy a gift for Mair, and decided the best place to go to get quality goods would be a Jewish shop. I looked in the window of the shop, saw what I liked and went in to see if I could manage some successful negotiations. For some reason I was quite excited about the fact that I was going into a real Jewish shop.

A young woman came forward to serve me and we began to talk about the item I had seen in the window. When her brother-in-law then came and joined the conversation I felt strongly constrained to say something quite unusual, "In actual fact the main reason I have come into this shop is because it is owned by Jews and I have such a respect and regard for the Jewish people." Of course they were surprised and no doubt did not hear this kind of remark from many customers. At that point a brother joined the group, so there were four of us looking at this item.

One of them asked, "Why did you say that?" "Because I am a Christian and as Christians we greatly respect the Jewish nation. We recognize Jews are the children of God and that they have had and still have a special role to play in the purposes of God," I replied. Again there was a look of surprise on their faces. I added "And I know that God's blessing is upon you as a nation and though you go through difficult, trying and hard times it does not change the fact that God's blessing is still upon you as a nation." Pleased about this, the brothers remarked to one another "You know this man is really serious". As we talked the mother, who owned the business, came out of the office. Now we were five.

When I said, "The greatest thing that could ever happen to you is to recognize Jesus Christ as the Messiah", one of the brothers spoke up, "But we could never become Christians, because of what you believe. You believe in reincarnation." I assured him we did not, but he insisted, "You do, you definitely do. You believe that you have to be born again." This was an interpretation I had never encountered before! "No, no, it's not your flesh and body being born again it's the you inside that God says must have a completely new start in life—in other words be born again."

One of the brothers looked earnestly at me and, with arms outstretched and palms turned upwards towards me, said to me with deep sincerity, in the words of Nicodemus in John 3:4, "How can a man be born again?" It was possibly one of the most awesome experiences I've ever had when witnessing for Christ. I stood there thinking, "Lord Jesus, I'm standing where you stood." It was such an honour and privilege and, of course, it gave me the opportunity to explain the gospel of Jesus Christ. It was marvellous.

There are no limits to what God's Holy Spirit will do when we take the simple step of faith and witness. Arriving home we received a publication detailing how a group of Messianic believers were planning to start an evangelistic drive in the very city where this Jewish shop was. I phoned them and told them the story. They took the name and address of the shop and assured me that they would do everything possible to continue sharing the gospel with that family.

To encourage you to witness and not be afraid, I must tell the story of what happened to me on one occasion more recently when I visited the dentist. When I was in the middle of treatment the dentist's mobile phone rang. "Please excuse me," he apologized," my daughter-in-law is expecting twins and one of them is very ill and it's likely that the illness will affect the second baby and both will die." He told me that, although the twins were both still alive, the prognosis for the sick twin was not good. I expressed my sadness to hear this, especially as these were his first grandchildren, but as I was going home the Lord spoke to me quite clearly and said, "Pray for those babies." Mair and I did pray together very specially that the Lord would miraculously undertake and these twins would be born in good health.

Returning to the surgery for my next appointment, I enquired how the twins were. His exact words were, "Well, it's quite amazing! On the day you were here, in fact that afternoon, suddenly the sick baby became well. They are still unborn but they are both well."

I had attempted to speak about the Lord to him before but he had completely rejected any thought of the reality of God, but now I was able to explain that on my way home that day I had felt God say to me that my wife and I should specially pray for the twins and that was what we had done, asking God to heal the sick twin. "My goodness, you must have a contact up there then," he responded and we were able to talk about how, by believing in Christ, we have a contact with God.

On my third appointment the dentist himself opened the door and stood with his right arm outstretched to shake my hand, "Thank you very much. It's amazing—those babies have been born fit and healthy. You really must have a contact up there!" We praised God for answered prayer.

It's worthwhile witnessing in the most difficult situations, even when you are faced with total unbelief. I assure you, you will know without a doubt that God is standing by you.

In recent years I have been greatly helped by the teaching of Tony Anthony of Avanti Ministries. During one of his seminars on evangelism he makes it clear that the task God has given us when witnessing as believers is not to be pressing people to make a decision for Christ. Our task is to proclaim the gospel at every possible opportunity and in every conceivable way. Yes, just proclaim the gospel. It is God who saves, for he is the God of the harvest and his Word will not return to him void. This releases us from any sense of failure if we are not seeing immediate results.

CHAPTER 12 ▬▬▬▬▬▬▬▬▬

More Revelation Giving, Prophecy and a Miracle

By this time we had a congregation of some thirty people who, like our previous congregations in Aberdeen and Glasgow, had never heard of giving by revelation. We needed £2000 to send a new convert to Bible College. I assured them that, if they would follow our guidance on revelation giving, we would have that figure in one offering. Many laughed through unbelief. On Sunday, when the offering was taken, the two elders went out to count it. No one present can ever forget the look on their faces when they returned. They announced that the offering came to £2,005. Praise the Lord! The same happened when we launched the Building Fund and the congregation was still the same size. I felt sure God had said the figure was £5,000. It was, and we received it in a single offering one Sunday morning.

Revelation giving is an amazing way to give and the result is that all who are involved are blessed in a way they have never experienced before. We expanded on our first experiences of this in Aberdeen, always teaching that it is taken for granted that believers tithe, otherwise a portion of their revelation giving is only a part of their tithes. The blessing of revelation giving follows givers through their lives as they continue in this practice and we had already proved this in previous situations.

Revelation giving must not be confused with extreme health, wealth and prosperity teaching. We simply follow Scripture, without any ulterior motive of giving for what we can get in return, but as a result we see other scriptures being fulfilled in our lives and God blessing both spiritually and materially. Paul speaks to the Corinthians about this matter:

> Remember that the person who plants few seeds will have a small crop; the one who plants many seeds will have a large crop. You should each give, then, as you have decided, not with regret or out of a sense of duty; for God loves the one who gives gladly. And God is able to give you more than you need, so that you will always have all you need for yourselves and more than enough for every good cause. As the scripture says, "He gives generously to the needy; his kindness lasts forever." And God, who supplies seed for the sower and bread to eat, will also supply you with all the seed you need and will make it grow and produce a rich harvest from your generosity. He will always make you rich enough to be generous at all times, so that many will thank God for your gifts which they

> receive from us. For this service you perform not only meets the needs of God's people, but also produces an outpouring of gratitude to God. 2 Cor. 9:6-12 (GNB)

The first principle of revelation giving is that Christians should not live on maximum budget, spending up to the last penny every month. Living on maximum budget makes it impossible to respond to God's promptings to give, even though we want to. The problem is that we have not arranged our finances in the way Paul shows us. Paul teaches that God will always give believers what they need—not want! If we live according to what we need rather than what we want, (and that does not mean living in a penny-pinching way), then we will have "more than enough for every good cause." It is correct and proper for a Christian to have a bank account and a good balance in it. This is to be ready and able to give to the causes that God brings to our notice. All our finances are "Kingdom finances" and we are only custodians of them.

Take this normal church scenario: The leader makes an appeal for a certain figure for a particular need. He gives the congregation opportunity to prepare to give, often using the phrase, "we will take up an offering". People look to see what they have in their pockets and give accordingly, but should God's work be brought down to the level of scraping together money from here or there? Often our reasoning goes like this: "I've got this much. I need this much for such and such and then I'd better keep a bit just in case. What have I left? I'll offer that to God!" Surely this way of thinking does not honour God. We need a revelation of what God wants us to give.

In revelation giving we pray and ask God for a figure and this is exciting. God will give you a figure which may well disappoint you, because you were ready to give more. Do not give a penny more. God knows why he gave you that figure. It is possible that the remaining monies you have are for another cause. On the other hand, the figure may be more than you expected—even much more! Do not give a penny less or you will miss your blessing. When the congregation is given opportunity to pray and everybody is obedient, we have experienced that, on every occasion, the giving has reached the target.

The same adventure can be experienced between husbands and wives. It is quite remarkable. What Mair and I do is we both write our figure on a piece of paper, then pass the paper to each other. What joy and laughter this brings and you will look forward to the next time you are challenged to give.

What is the outcome of revelation giving?

> And God, who supplies seed to sow and bread to eat, will also supply you with all the seed you need and will make it grow and produce a rich harvest from your generosity. He will always make you rich enough to be generous at all times, so that many will thank God for your gifts which they receive from us. 2 Corinthians 9:10,11

For us, that is what Christian living is all about.

In Inverness Christian Fellowship we realized the need to help the poor, so we developed a Faith In Action Team. On more than a dozen occasions in the New Testament there is reference to good works being essential for the believer to do. Jesus says it and so do the apostles, so it is important for us to get this message.

I observe that the call to good works has resulted in two extreme responses. On the one hand, in some circles, we see Christians developing a social gospel and neglecting the spiritual challenges. On the other hand we see Christians emphasizing "not of works lest any man should boast" (Eph. 2:9) to a point where they ignore the challenge of practical, good works. This results in God being robbed of glory, because Jesus says, "that they may see your good works and glorify your Father who is in heaven." (Matt. 5:16). The church that has got it right is the church that is doing both the spiritual and the practical.

The Faith In Action team would go round painting or cleaning peoples' homes and giving them gifts of furniture. We recognized when we went into this kind of ministry that we would from time to time be taken advantage of, but that did not deter us. Few escape that painful experience. We learned to laugh!

There were also positive outcomes. On one occasion a team went in to paint a woman's house because it was in a desperate state. That woman came to know the Lord and she continues to follow him many years later. Many other such examples made it all worthwhile.

Our team had an old Ford minibus with the seats taken out. It still had all its windows, which was a problem as people could see the furniture and white goods inside. The team worked in very poor and rough areas of the community and unexpected things would happen. One evening the van broke down! The team did everything in their power to try and restart it, but it refused to go. Because it was an old van, the doors didn't even lock, so a van full of fridges, cookers, and furniture had to be left unsecured overnight.

Everyone anticipated that, when they returned next morning to tow it away, the van would be empty for sure! But, looking through the windows, there wasn't a single thing missing and lying on the front passenger seat was the broken part of the engine! Someone had come from that housing estate, taken out the broken part and replaced it with a new part, leaving the old part on the seat. The team turned the key and instantly the engine started and from then on they had no further problems. Wasn't that a tremendous way for people to show their gratitude? It also taught us a lesson in relation to judging people. The experience was a wonderful encouragement for the team who worked so hard in that housing estate. God honours good works.

Prophecy has played a very significant part in our life and ministry and I have seen so many specific prophecies fulfilled it is hard to know which to recount. Before we came to Inverness as pioneers, the Lord spoke through Eric Horley, a recognized prophet, at the Apostolic Church International Convention of 1987. He gave me two specific words of prophecy in the presence of 1,800 people. The first was that on going to the Highlands I would stand in front of an altar and declare the vision that was dear to my heart. I was doubtful about this prophecy, knowing that churches in Scotland don't have altars! But I had forgotten about the Episcopalian churches.

A year after arriving in Inverness, an Episcopalian priest asked me to speak on Whit Sunday in his church. Where did I stand? In front of the altar! What did I speak about? The vision dear to my heart, that God has made His Spirit available to every believer and that we can be filled with the Spirit of God with signs following. All we have to do is to ask according to his Word and by his grace we will enter into a new and deep relationship with our Lord.

> If you then, being evil, know how to give good
> gifts to your children, how much more will
> your heavenly Father give the Holy Spirit to
> those who ask Him? Luke 11:13

Eric Horley's other prophecy about our mission was: "You will receive invitations and although stained glass windows will be there, you will stand and I will anoint you and they will receive the truth." This second prophecy was fulfilled when, in 1989, I went to St Peter's Church of Scotland in Wick. As I preached, I was facing one of the biggest stained glass windows you will ever see in a local church! Such experiences establish a deep assurance in our hearts that God speaks today and is interested in everything we do in his Name. Fulfilled prophecy also creates a confidence in God to be ready at all times to step out of the box and trust him.

One Saturday night at an interdenominational service, during the time of worship, I distinctly and suddenly saw a specific place on the road to the island of Skye. In fact it was the rocks at Sheil Bridge. At first I thought it was my imagination because I was going to preach in Skye the next morning. Then the voice said, "There will be a man standing near the rocks. You must give him a lift." I carried on enjoying the worship but the word came back again and I remember saying, "Alright Lord, I'll give him a lift."

I thought no more about it. As Mair remained behind to lead worship in Inverness, I left for Skye at 8am the next morning on my own. On that road early in the morning there is never a soul in sight. I have often counted only twelve to fifteen cars in seventy miles and have seldom seen a person on the road in the entire one hundred and twenty-five mile trip. I came to the spot at Sheil Bridge some sixty miles from home.

Sure enough, there was a man standing, thumbing a lift. He looked unkempt, to be polite, and I confess I did drive past him. Then the Lord said to me, "You promised to give him a lift!" I stopped, reversed and he got into the car. He said he was going to climb the Cuillin hills in Skye. We began to talk. He had strange but remarkably deep insights into the spiritual state of the Highlanders in relation to the gospel. This was peculiar because he said he came from Canada. He then said, "You see, they will have spiritual difficulties because they do not understand that sin is not a part of the original human nature. It is an appendage to it." I nearly let go of the steering wheel because that was precisely the last line in the sermon notes that I was taking to preach in Skye. I felt the nature of the phrase was unusual—it was not a common phrase like "God loves you." I will never forget that journey. When we came to Broadford, a village on Skye, I prayed with him before he left the car, then he was gone. When I travel that way I often look back on that experience and thank God for the revelation he brought.

Without a doubt God speaks through pictures and visions, but because so many are now being presented to individuals and groups of people in the Body of Christ, I think there is room for caution. I have listened to the strangest pictures being described, such as "I see a geranium blossoming in the middle of nowhere," or "I see water going over a water wheel backwards." Most of the people giving these visions then say "I present this to you. Has anyone an interpretation of this vision?" By doing this they are absolving themselves of all responsibility for what they have brought to the group. This distresses me greatly as each of us must take responsibility for our own actions and words.

I am very aware of the dreams and visions that Joseph had, as recorded in Genesis, but I do see the problems they created for him when not handled properly. I am also aware Joel says "Your old men will dream dreams, your young men will see visions" (Joel 2:28). I am not disbelieving regarding these matters, but I know the church needs some guidance on this subject because many lives are being upset and thrown into confusion due to private and uncensored pictures and visions. I have recently had two telephone calls from people outside of the churches I superintend that are in serious confusion because of this problem.

I believe that the gifts of the Holy Spirit, wherever possible are to operate under the covering of local church leadership. I can see no license in scripture for people giving private prophecies, pictures or visions without the cover of the leadership. It is far too easy to be riding the wave of some emotional high, and be carried away by zeal or a search for kudos to give prophecies of great promise that elate for the moment but leave bewilderment in the future.

When there was a rise of this phenomenon in Inverness Christian Fellowship I sought the Lord for some guidance and remain grateful beyond words for the outcome. The thought that was put into my mind was this, "What was the first kind of book you ever had?" Immediately I said to myself "A picture book." The next question was "What was the second kind of book you had?" I thought, "A book with words and pictures." "What was the third kind of book you had?" "A book with only words." This immediately put a new light on to the whole matter.

Although pictures and visions are undoubtedly scriptural it was clearly my responsibility, as a pastor, to encourage people to grow by waiting on God so that revelation would flow out of a deepening relationship with him. I counselled them that when they received a picture they ask God for an understanding of what they had received. Just like the second kind of book I used to have. It showed me a picture of a cat and the word "cat" was underneath it. Then, in order to progress in God and in the life of the Spirit, I encouraged them to wait further on God to allow Him to develop their prophetic gift.

They needed to move on from receiving a picture to receiving a prophetic word from the Lord. That is book three—a book with words, but no pictures. Very often pictures just come on the spur of the moment, but a gift of prophecy demands much time spent before God. It is during those times of waiting that the seeds of prophetic words are deposited in the person and the church is enriched.

There were in our fellowship in Inverness several people who worked in the local hospital. One day a senior nurse belonging to the church asked me if I would come to the hospital and pray for a young man who had been in a coma for over three weeks. His mother was a Christian and had sat beside his bed every day since his accident. Arriving in the hospital I met the mother and her eldest daughter. Though the boy's condition was very serious, the mother had never lost faith that her son would be healed. I looked into his vacant eyes and his body seemed very small as it was rolled up in the bed.

It was easier to talk to the family than generate faith to go and pray for the boy; so that is what I did. I knew in the end I had to go over to the bed and pray, but sometimes it is so difficult. The accident had been so serious that the brain damage was severe and the prognosis was extremely disheartening. Even if he ever regained consciousness he would need to learn to walk again, as well as to read and write.

Eventually I summoned enough faith to go and pray. I spoke to the lad, understanding that people in a coma can hear even though they cannot respond. Eventually while still speaking to this motionless body, I mentioned the name of Jesus. Suddenly the young man leapt out of bed. At this point I discovered he was nearly six foot tall and very well built. He went for my throat with both hands. I quickly grabbed his forearms and called out, "In the name of Jesus come out of him." He fell back into the bed, turned over and went to sleep. Amazingly, within three days he was home with his family.

He never did need to learn to walk again or learn to read and write. God had performed a double miracle at that moment beside the bed. He was delivered and healed at the same time. Today he is a husband and the father of three lovely children. He is also a leader in the church that was birthed because of this miracle. When I am preaching in that little church I often look at the scar on his neck where the tracheotomy was during his illness. Even although it was several years ago the wonder of it all sweeps over my heart and I worship God.

CHAPTER 13 ▰▰▰▰▰▰▰▰▰

Deliverance and Healings

In Inverness occult fairs were regularly held. As Christians we would go and stand outside in groups, quietly praying and distributing literature to those going in. Because of the presence of Christians praying, throughout the day the mediums would come out and put their arms round trees and pray to them calling for their spirit guides to make contact. Our silent praying was very effective, to the point that on one occasion the spiritualists called the police and asked them to remove us because they could not contact their spirit guides.

One day I saw a young lady and her mother approaching the fair. I was compelled to speak to them. I gave them some literature that warned them of the dangers of attending such events. I turned to the younger lady and told her God understood that she was going into the fair because she was seeking help about her marriage. God knew that the marriage was in difficulty and he knew the pain she was going through. I also told her about the adverse effect this was having on the children. They asked how I knew all this. "Because God told me and this is proof that He loves you and wants to help you," I replied. They agreed that all I said was true, thanked me, and never went into the fair. They also indicated that they would speak to God about the situation. I can only trust that they did just that.

It is interesting to reflect on how the church in Britain, by failing to operate in the gifts of the Spirit has created a market for the occult! Please do not quickly brush this matter aside with a sigh and some expression of regret for the state of affairs that prevails at present in the Body of Christ. It is our bounden duty as believers to very seriously respond to the call of God to "desire earnestly spiritual gifts" (1Cor.14:1). There is placed in the hearts of men and women who are not following Christ—a desire, even perhaps an expectation, to see the miraculous. I think of the crowds that flock to see weeping statues, the many that visit fortune tellers and spiritualists and "faith" healers to name but a few. Oh Church of Christ arise to the call and the invitation to receive spiritual gifts!

Before I recount this next story of deliverance I want you to know that the name of Jesus is all powerful and that this ministry is for those who believe. It is also my sincere belief that it is very dangerous for a church to be moving on in God without someone in that church, preferably in the leadership, operating the gift of the discerning of spirits. You will notice from Christ's ministry that on several occasions when a sick person came to him he did not pray for their healing but cast out a demon. How many of us have prayed for the healing of a person when all along the problem was not sickness? I have referred to one or two cases already and there have been many others.

I would appeal to you not to attempt this ministry on your own, but rather under the cover of one of your church leaders who has the gift of discerning of spirits. There are so many pitfalls to encounter when operating in this ministry that it is essential to have an experienced person with you, at least for the first few occasions. Make sure there are always two of you when ministering in this way. It was not by chance that Jesus "sent them two and two ahead of him into every city and place" (Luke 10:1).

There are great blessings that ensue from the ministry of deliverance. The main one is that you will understand, more than ever before, the reality of Jesus' Lordship when you see it in action. It will be a permanent experience locked into your mind that will change your whole spiritual thinking.

On a visit to Southern Ireland I encountered a young man, brought up in the Catholic Church, who had given his life to the Lord and was having times when his service for the Lord showed fruit, but then he would go into times of total defeat. We prayed for him and one by one many demons left him until once again the last and by far the most powerful demon was being confronted. We could not move it.

Leaving my colleague to continue to pray over the man, I went to the corner of the room to pray. I never want to forget what the Spirit said to me. He said, "A blessing in darkness is a curse in light!'" From that I understood that some very powerful person who was in darkness had blessed this man at some time in the past. In fact it was a priest who had prayed over him as a child at the request of his grandmother. Returning to his side I spoke it out as God had shown me. The young man levitated and suddenly fell to the floor completely delivered. Today that man is serving God as a full time evangelist in Canada.

The next incident concerns vegetarianism and you may think that what I have to say is extreme, but I believe, unless it is for reasons of taste or medical necessity, Christians should not be vegetarians. Vegetarianism is closely linked to the teaching of eastern religions, which is something Christians are to avoid.

The apostle Paul tells us:

> But the Spirit explicitly says that in later times some will fall away from the faith, paying attention to deceitful spirits and doctrines of demons, by means of the hypocrisy of liars seared in their own consciences as with a branding iron, men who forbid marriage and advocate abstaining from foods which God has created to be gratefully shared in by those who believe and know the truth. For everything created by God is good, and nothing is to be rejected if it is received with thanksgiving. 1Tim.4:1-4

In Inverness a young woman, who was a vegetarian and came from a New Age commune, committed her life to Christ. It was a great day when she met with the church leaders to be set free. On this occasion when we prayed for her a demon began to scream. By the power of the name of Jesus she was delivered and sat on the settee shouting, "I want meat, I want meat!" She has continued to rejoice in her deliverance to this day. However, I am not for one minute suggesting that every vegetarian is demonized. Not at all! This was a very unique case.

On another occasion there was a young man who had heard about us giving away furniture, so he contacted one of our team to ask if we would be able to provide some for him, as he had very little. Our team went in and gave him just what he was looking for. They then witnessed to him about the Lord and eventually brought him to a service. Much to our surprise from time to time he became quite angry and vocal in the services and his eyes would bulge when the gospel was preached. It was a very difficult time. At times he would stand up in a service and run out shouting. By this behaviour we recognized the demonic. Demons cannot rest in the presence of the Lord. As we came to know this young man better he invited us to his home, as he too realized that he was possessed by many demons.

I took another young man, a new convert, with me to the man's home. I knew this would be good experience for him and he could pray with me. Neither of these men had seen demons cast out. In fact the new believer was convinced I was only exacerbating the situation and did not even believe in the existence of demons. That misconception did not last for long! When we began to pray the man suddenly began to leap violently from one chair to another and we had to follow him round his home. He finally fell to the floor and after several smaller demons came out of him, out came what I am inclined to call the "parent" demon—the main demon that had filled the man's life and controlled it. When the young convert saw this one coming out he then knew that we were being confronted with real demonic power because of other evidence that it is better not to mention. We saw in undeniable terms that the power of the name of Jesus was almighty. It was a truly awesome moment.

From there on that young man became normal and happy and really came to love the Lord. He fell in love with God's word and he would read his Bible day and night because it was blessing him and giving him authority over the powers of darkness in which he had been so heavily involved.

We eventually learned that he had been one of a group of people who were from the house that a man named Crowley had owned. Crowley was one of the founders of certain forms of occultism in Britain. His house, which is down at the side of Loch Ness, has tunnels in it leading to a graveyard where they held feasts and festivals. The young man who had been delivered began to tell us a little of the goings on. He was too afraid to tell everything because his former associates came to hear that he was converted and that he had relinquished all connections with occultism and he received very serious, life threatening letters. It was a difficult situation, but he stood strong and believed God for protection. It had been a very deep and dark past that to us was quite a revelation, especially when he spoke of his powers to curse that he could use at will.

During his time in this occult group he had worn robes to fulfill his role in the satanic worship ceremonies. One day he came to me and said, "I've got a lot of stuff. I've got clothes, these gowns and I've got books and other stuff all attached to my occult days and I want to get rid of them." The only answer was to burn them and we involved the

Fellowship so that other Christians could come and unite in support of him.

We arranged, one summer evening, to go down the east side of Loch Ness after a Sunday service. There are several places where it is possible to stop and stand on the shore of the Loch. I drove past one or two of these places and eventually pulled in. "We'll do it on this spot," I signalled and we parked the cars. Over twenty people had come. When he asked me why I had chosen this particular place I replied, "I don't know. I just felt this was the right spot to make the bonfire." "Well," he said, "Can you believe this? This is the spot where I, with others, held my last occult ceremony with burning candles and all that accompanies it?"

We gathered all the paraphernalia out of the boot of the car, carried it over to the stones on the shore, set it all up and had a time of prayer and worship before we lit the fire. Very soon there was an enormous fire, with the flames rising high into the air. It was a memorable sight. We were standing there glorifying God and declaring the power of the blood of Christ. It was such a wonderful time of praising God. He too was praising God as he realized that this was the end of his old life.

As the fire was burning we watched it gradually die down a little and I saw in the middle of the fire a packet which was completely untouched by the flames that were all around it. It wasn't even singed. I got a stick from somewhere and gave it a poke. There in a box untouched by the flames was a pack of tarot cards. We could not believe this and so I poked it and poked it and pushed it and shoved it, until in the end the packet burst open and out came all the cards.

We were singing and declaring the power of the blood and the Lordship of Christ. Suddenly these cards burst into flames. We were astonished at the multi-coloured flames that suddenly rose from those burning cards. Although I cannot explain what was happening, I don't think it had anything to do with the ink on the cards. I will never forget the purples and oranges and the greens that were rising up in high flames in the middle of the fire. Eventually every card was burned and the people were rejoicing and praising God. It was one of the most powerful meetings that we had held. Those men and women present came to understand as never before the reality of the powers of darkness but they witnessed in an unforgettable way that Jesus Christ is Lord over them all.

During our time in Inverness we also witnessed outstanding cases of divine healing. Dolina Geddes had a chronic back problem. On a Sunday of prayer and fasting, she asked for prayer because she had lost all sensation in her foot and ankle. Her doctor had told her because of this and other medical reasons she must hand in her driving license. Given the need for prayer, we gathered round her and called on God. It was a thing to behold; she shook in a very frightening way, and then began to weep. When she settled down, she found that feeling had been restored to her foot and ankle! She has never had a problem again. Nobody present on that day will ever forget that moment of divine intervention.

I experienced an outstanding healing of my own. One day when driving the car a voice said clearly, "No knife will touch your throat." Shock, gratitude and bewilderment overcame me, but in a couple of months I forgot all about it. About two or three months later I woke one morning with unbearable pain in my mouth. It was so severe I was literally banging my head on the wall to distract me from the pain. The doctor sent me to Raigmore Hospital in Inverness with a diagnosis of stones in my salivary duct. Now I remembered! Firstly I remembered about the voice, then about an episode in Glasgow many years before when I had previously suffered with stones in that duct. A doctor at Glasgow Royal Infirmary had operated under local anesthetic and removed the stones. He warned me that if it happened again, I would need an operation on the salivary gland, which was dangerously near an important facial nerve. It was all coming together!

I sat in the waiting area of the hospital and thanked God in faith for the promise that he had given me. Suddenly I slightly choked and coughed and brought something up. I put my cupped hands to my mouth and they filled with saliva, some blood and two big calcium stones. People were staring at me! I called a nurse who exclaimed in a loud voice, "Get a doctor!" He came, inspected what was in my cupped hands and said, "This is a miracle. Those stones are bigger than the duct and they could not have come out by themselves." I do not pretend to understand medicine, but I do know that God always keeps His Word! we give him all the glory.

For four years we held Highland Conventions which were called "Highland Harvest." Each year we sensed and saw the presence of God at work. During the 2001 Highland Harvest convention in Portree, Isle of Skye, we were enjoying a remarkable time of praise and worship, led by the worship group Resound, when the inner voice of the Lord told me to go and pray for a lady with crutches. I did not know her, but had noticed her coming into the Convention. The worship continued and while everyone was praising the Lord, I quietly slipped over to the woman and prayed for her healing. Immediately she jumped up and began to dance and rejoice in the Lord.

Later in the service, a woman came forward with a revelation that someone present had severe migraine headaches. The person that had just been healed announced that it was her. Others gathered round the woman, and prayed for her healing. She had suffered from Myalgic Encephalomyelitis (M.E.) for years. On several occasions because of it she had been bedridden. At this time she was a little more mobile and so came to the Convention on crutches. That day God completely healed her.

I know all this because a few weeks later she asked Mair and me to visit. Her question was, "Now I am completely healed, what shall I do about my disability allowance?" It was about four hundred pounds per month and she had no other form of income. My reaction was a little cautious. I told her it was a bit drastic to surrender her means of living. Perhaps she should wait a little while to be sure that her healing was complete. At this she got quite upset, telling me she did not want that sort of advice from a pastor. She said that she already knew what she had to do in faith, but only needed confirmation! I was suitably rebuked by her greater faith. In faith she cancelled the benefit and within weeks she was jogging every morning! Today she is a drug rehabilitation worker in one of our Scottish cities. She has never had recurrence of M.E. or a migraine since she was prayed for that day.

These are but some of the cases in which I have been privileged to see God at work in a powerful and awesome way. People who were sick are now living in health and serving the Lord free of pain and disability. The delivered have peace of mind and enjoy the blessing of his presence in their lives. The thrill is that in the ministry of deliverance there is the guarantee of a one hundred percent success because Jesus is Lord. In the case of healing it is different, because there is the mystery of Divine Sovereignty. No one can claim that all cases are immediately healed, and some we may never see healed.

As we put these incidents of healing and deliverance together, surely there is a longing birthed in our hearts to be a part of a gospel that reflects the one we read of in the book of Acts—the gospel that people said they "saw" as well as "heard"? I am not deluded into thinking that everybody who sees or experiences a miracle will immediately surrender their lives to Christ. Sadly I have seen proof of the opposite. Yet Jesus has by his death brought a salvation that, as he clearly demonstrated, touches body as well as spirit. It is not ours to establish what the outcome is of the miraculous. All I know is that it is a part of the gospel and God has not removed it from the New Covenant.

CHAPTER 14 ▮▮▮▮▮▮▮▮▮▮▮▮

Passing on the Baton

My ministry in Inverness Christian Fellowship finished in 1995, although I remain involved in the Highland Network and retain oversight for this group of fellowships, travelling to support, preach and teach.

As in a relay race each person is responsible for holding on tightly to the baton and running the complete length of his section before passing it securely to the next person in the team, so it is in the Christian life:

> Therefore, since we have so great a cloud of witnesses surrounding us, let us also lay aside every encumbrance and the sin which so easily entangles us, and let us run with endurance the race that is set before us, fixing our eyes on Jesus, the author and perfecter of faith, who for the joy set before Him endured the cross, despising the shame, and has sat down at the right hand of the throne of God. For consider

> Him who has endured such hostility by sinners against Himself, so that you will not grow weary and lose heart. Hebrews 12:1

Alongside our individual responsibility before God we also have an essential part to play in our local church and in the Body of Christ and we are accountable to them. It is with this in mind that I close with two further comments: one relating to the church and the equipping of its leaders and the other to each of us as individuals.

I am beginning to discover there are certain important teachings for the Body of Christ which bring real and relevant experiences for believers in God. Sadly, due to reasons not mine to give, I seem to see them slipping into history and of course it is a great loss for the Body of Christ, because all the teachings of the New Testament are important.

As I look at the ministries in the Church of Christ I compare them to vitamins in a healthy body. We need a balance of vitamins, some more than others, but all essential. We cannot live on just one vitamin. Very often it seems as though there is one vitamin that is predominant—that of preaching. It is a great ministry to the Body of Christ giving strength and growth and creating godly aspirations, but there are many, many other ministries. Even if we look at the ministries of Ephesians 4:11 surely these are very powerful vitamins required for the Body of Christ and each differs from the others.

> Therefore it says, 'When he ascended on high, he led captive a host of captives, and he gave gifts to men. . . . . And He gave some as apostles, and

> some as prophets, and some as evangelists, and
> some as pastors and teachers. Ephesians 4:8,11

The ministry of an apostle is entirely different to the ministry of an evangelist and the ministry of an evangelist is very different to the ministry of a teacher and so on. But we need them all, every single one of them, for the Body to be healthy. If we do not have evangelists teaching us how to evangelize we are gradually going to decline. And men whose ministry is to prophesy have a totally distinct ministry to the Bible teacher.

As we look into scripture we see that God has married two ministries in relation to the Church,

> having been built on the foundation of the
> apostles and prophets, Christ Jesus Himself
> being the corner stone. Eph. 2:20

Now you may have a vision of the Church of Christ as a skyscraper—one building, on one foundation, built by the apostles and prophets of the first century. I am totally convinced God was not attempting to create that thought in our minds. Whenever and wherever the church is being established, it is established on Christ the corner stone and the foundational ministries of present day apostles and prophets.

It was after the ascension of Christ, when he had been appointed head over all things to the Church, that he gave the five ministries to men, which in fact are the composite ministries of Christ. As in the physical, so in the spiritual, the abilities resident in the head are expressed through the body.

> These are in accordance with the working of
> the strength of His might which He brought
> about in Christ, when He raised Him from
> the dead and seated Him at His right hand
> in the heavenly places, far above all rule and
> authority and power and dominion, and every
> name that is named, not only in this age but
> also in the one to come. And He put all things
> in subjection under His feet, and gave Him as
> head over all things to the church, which is His
> body, the fullness of Him who fills all in all.
> Eph. 1:19-23

Because it was after Christ ascended that he gave these five ministries to the church, we read of some nineteen apostles in the New Testament. Therefore the foundation ministry of apostles and prophets continues in every nation and generation, wherever the church is being built. The Church needs in the foundation the married ministries of apostles and prophets working as one together. We see an example of this in the Apostle Paul's life:

> But Paul chose Silas and left, being committed
> by the brethren to the grace of the Lord.
> Acts 15:40

On his second missionary journey, he takes with him Silas, "Judas and Silas, also being prophets themselves." (Acts 15:32) Paul and Silas went together. It is very interesting to note that the second missionary journey was the most outstanding of his three journeys. This was when they moved into the new area of establishing Gentile churches wherever they went.

It became clear at the commencement of the Apostolic Church that these twinned ministries brought a powerful, enlightening and enriching experience to the fellowship. There have been, and still are, occasions in my life when I have clearly witnessed the fact that apostle and prophet ministries are truly spiritually married.

I remember going down once to minister to our church in Clydebank, just outside Glasgow, taking with me a prophet. I had prepared some ministry for this group of people and, during the time of prayer, before I began to preach, the prophet began to prophesy. It was hard to believe what I was listening to. You could honestly have thought the prophet had written my notes for the sermon. He actually started by saying, "I want to speak to you tonight about your inheritance". I pulled the notes out of my Bible because the heading of it was "Your Inheritance", and I passed the notes along the platform to show all the leaders that this man was actually prophesying my message.

We had come to a point where this prophet and I had become so "as one" spiritually that, as we travelled together ministering, such confirmations frequently happened. The substance of the prophecies was precisely what the Lord was giving me to speak to the people about. However, this does not duplicate ministry, but rather confirms it. It is another vitamin bringing the health to the Body of Christ in an entirely different way. The emphasis is greatly enriched by the fact that the Holy Spirit has revealed the same issues through the different ministries of apostle and prophet, with each being unaware of this.

On another memorable occasion in one of the villages in the Highlands an apostle and prophet were invited to come and minister to a small congregation. Leading the meeting I had no idea the battle the apostle had gone through regarding what to preach on, but, at the end of the time of prayer, the prophet who was sitting in the congregation got up and walked down the aisle to the front and stood at the lectern. He began the prophetic word by saying, "As I directed my servant Micah as you read it in Micah 1:6" and he recited:

> For I will make Samaria a heap of ruins in the
> open country, planting places for a vineyard. I
> will pour her stones down into the valley, and
> will lay bare her foundations.

This is not a scripture which is frequently read. The prophet recited it and continued to prophesy.

After he had finished speaking I made no comment on the prophecy, but in prayer I thanked God for the prophetic word, knowing that the apostle that was with this prophet would handle it in his ministry. The apostle stood up and explained that he was totally overwhelmed and would never, ever forget the experience. He had been struggling greatly about this message the Lord had given him on Micah 1:6. He was telling the Lord that he could not bring this ministry in this church because these were godly people and he would just like to bring a word of encouragement and comfort. But he knew he had to minister on Micah 1 starting at verse 6 and this was a powerful confirmation through the prophet.

Here was another wonderful example of God marrying the ministries of apostle and prophet. These men are disciplined and do not discuss their ministries with each other prior to the occasion. The loss of this dual ministry in the Church is a loss it cannot afford because this ministry is foundational.

God's household, having been built upon the foundation of the apostles and prophets, Christ Jesus Himself being the cornerstone Ephesians 2:19b, 20

Such confirmation is not only a source of strength to the Church, it is also a source of strength to the apostles and the prophets themselves. A long time ago one of the founding fathers of the Apostolic Church said that a strong apostle creates a strong prophet and in the very same way a strong prophet will strengthen an apostle who is perhaps hesitant.

It is vital that such fundamental New Testament truths are not lost because we need a healthy Church in this day of continual onslaught. We are living in a day when truth is being eroded and standards are being lowered lest we cause offence. If ever there were a day for the re-establishing of truth, this is the day.

Therefore, for many years, it has been one of my deep desires to make sure that our generation ensures the next generation is well trained and equipped to serve the Lord. Over time I had several different opportunities to promote this vision and finally in 1999 an opening came to work with three colleagues to set up the Ministry Development Programme in the Apostolic Church Bible College in South Wales. It is now called "IMPACT" and runs from a Scottish base. The programme was launched nationally in our denomination and affiliated churches and it was the fulfillment of a long-held dream to see men and women registering for a two year distance learning course and through it receiving the essential foundations for Christian ministry.

The programme comprises four practical elements, which are leadership with teambuilding, pastoral care, missiology and preaching, together with eight theological appetizers. The practical emphasis became the real magnet and we have seen well over one hundred and fifty students completing the programme. It was very exciting to discover, when we concluded the first phase some ten years later, that more than forty young men and women had entered the ministry as a result.

Much to our surprise church leaders in Italy heard about this and in 2010, after an initial introductory programme, adopted the Ministry Development Programme for the Italian Apostolic Church nationally. There is nothing more rewarding than seeing young men and women committing themselves to study and prepare for God's service. I trust and pray that generation after generation will be ready to sacrifice their time and energy and talents to be engaged in the greatest message the world can ever hear—the message of the gospel of Jesus Christ.

My heart's desire is also for all God's people to clearly recognize the voice of God in their individual lives. It is an amazing fact that from time to time God synchronizes the thoughts of his people, preparing them for the preaching of the Word that will be brought to the church. For instance, whilst waiting on the Lord recently for a Sunday morning's sermon, he clearly spoke to me and told me the subject I had to speak on. I prepared my heart for that ministry. When I arrived at the church they had just concluded their prayer meeting in which they had received a prophecy quoting from the very Scripture I was to read and even revealing the subject I was to speak on. It was utterly amazing. Here was God speaking at different times and to different people about what He wished to emphasize that day in the lives of the congregation.

There is an interesting practice in that particular church in Skye. The church is held in a community centre and there is a blackboard on the wall. Every week one of the members writes on the blackboard when he arrives, 'Welcome to Skye Bible Church, Dunvegan' and underneath he puts a text. This particular Sunday the text actually gave the three points of the message the Lord had given me to preach. So here we have everyone involved in hearing what God is saying—the preacher and the congregation.

How did this come about? Were there claps of thunder and flashes of lightening or hailstones and the building shaking? Not at all! It was nothing more than a whispering thought and each person stepped out in faith, believed it was God and proceeded to speak it out. Over the years I have learned something very significant. I do believe that God speaks to all His children. Many think that when God speaks it has to come in some exceptional way and only to exceptional people. God is not limited in this way. He speaks by simple, gentle whispering thoughts to all believers and God calls us to follow it through as we recognize his voice amongst the thousands of other things and people that clamour for our attention.

Let us be encouraged by such stories. Every experience in our Christian life is a stepping stone and God is saying to us,

"Now take courage. Be reassured. I am speaking to you and it is my voice you are hearing." Of course the consequences of listening to those whispers and the blessings of obedience that follow are enormous.

Many times in this book I have dared to say that I have heard God speak to me. For many it may sound strange and for some it will sound as though I am setting myself up as a "super" Christian. This is furthest from my thoughts—I know myself! Still I cannot count how many times I have been asked by Christians how I can know it is God speaking to me and not just me imagining it. In the natural, we would all agree that the more we are in the company of a person the more familiar their voice becomes. I believe this is precisely the same in the spiritual realm. As we spend time with God we become more confident in recognizing his voice, increasing our capacity to receive from him. I am comforted by the words of Jesus who assured us that he would speak to us.

> My sheep hear My voice, and I know them, and
> they follow Me. John10:27

I believe that practicing God's presence is one sure way of learning to recognize his voice. How can we be sure it is God and not our own imaginations? What length will he go to in order to assure us it is his voice? I have found great help in reading from Peter's experience, when he was boasting that he would never fail God, never reject Jesus Christ and never turn away from confessing him as his Lord. Jesus spoke to him and said, "Before the cock crows you will deny me three times." That was an astonishing thing for Jesus to say and the disciples were totally bewildered.

There were rules and regulations put in place by the Jews that no cockerels were allowed to live in Jerusalem. Let me quote from a Jewish manuscript : "they do not bring up cocks in Jerusalem because of the holy things, neither do the priests in all the land of Israel because of the purifications." (Bava Kamma c.7, Section 7) This is verified by the fact that on one occasion a cockerel was found in Jerusalem and so it was written, ". . . nor can the Jews deny that there were cockerels at Jerusalem for they themselves spoke of a cock that was stoned at Jerusalem" (T. Hereos Erubin, fol. 26.1. Caphor, fol.42.1). They had found one in the city and stoned it to death keeping the city clear of cockerels. But Jesus said "Before the cock crows you will deny me three times." Would it not need a miracle for a cockerel to be there?

I think we are learning that when God wants to speak to us He will do anything to make sure that we know it is Him who is speaking. I remember once when serving as a pastor in Aberdeen and also in Peterhead, I was at the very end of my tether. During the Sunday morning worship service when I was kneeling to worship and praise God, but feeling absolutely brokenhearted deep inside, I suddenly found myself completely enveloped in brilliant sunshine. Although my eyes were closed I knew the sun was shining. I opened my eyes and against all the reality of the local weather conditions, through the window of the little church the sun shone right on to me and God spoke to me saying, "This is Me showing you that I am with you and I will always show you that I am with you when you are in deep distress by letting the sun shine."

That moment has never left me though it was more than thirty years ago because, from time to time through life when I have been confronted with very difficult situations, God has fulfilled that promise with a miracle. I know that for others he speaks by a rainbow, but you may find that for you it is something completely different, yet no less wonderful and reassuring.

On one occasion, when I had been asked to preach at a very large convention, I went away for a walk and the mist was very, very thick and very, very heavy. It was a long walk and I cried to God, "I can't go to this convention. I'm not able for this task. I'm asking you almighty God to come and help me and tell me whether I have a right to go or not. If you do not speak to me I cannot go." It is hard to believe, but, through the dense mist, the sun broke through and shone only at the spot where I was standing. It was a remarkable, astonishing experience—yet another for which to give God praise.

I remember telling a Christian farmer, who farmed in that area, about this experience and the day it happened. He said, "Samuel, that is an impossibility. The mist was so dense that day we could hardly see the cattle in the field." I assured him that this did happen. I went to that convention knowing that God had spoken by that sunbeam assurance that He would be with me.

But God has no favourites. Whoever we are and whenever we feel everything is against us or we face very difficult situations, God is ready to perform a miracle to speak into our lives. Just as Peter would never forget that somehow or other a cockerel got into Jerusalem and crowed precisely at the time when he was in his dilemma, so God is able to rearrange anything to make sure we know that He is speaking to us.

There are times when we feel we are on the verge of giving up. At that point only a word from God will take us through. It may be in a time of failure when we are sure that the Lord cannot forgive us again. Comfort from people is not enough, and we know we need God to speak. God is our Father and with a father's heart he will come in a firm and loving way, either by circumstances or by his voice, and he will speak. This is how I have come to know unswervingly that God is my Father and my friend.

EPILOGUE

Overall, one thing I have greatly appreciated is the gentle way the Lord led me step by step, on and on, from smaller things to bigger things and then into the very difficult situations. He did not drop me into the very difficult situations until I was ready for them. I pray that you will trust him to lead you, and by experience he will build up your faith.

> For My thoughts are not your thoughts, nor are your ways My ways, declares the LORD. For as the heavens are higher than the earth, so are My ways higher than your ways and My thoughts than your thoughts. For as the rain and the snow come down from heaven, and do not return there without watering the earth and making it bear and sprout, and furnishing seed to the sower and bread to the eater; so will My word be which goes forth from My mouth; it will not return to Me empty, without accomplishing what I desire, and without succeeding in the matter for which I sent it.
> Isaiah 55:8-11

Just as I stood at the beginning of my life as a wee boy singing a hymn in the open air, I conclude with the words of another hymn which, in every verse, reflects my life's experience:

Praise to the Lord, the Almighty, the King of
    creation!
O my soul, praise him, for he is thy health
    and salvation!
All ye who hear,
Brothers and sisters draw near;
Praise him in glad adoration.

Praise to the Lord, who doth prosper thy
    work and defend thee;
Surely his goodness and mercy here daily
    attend thee.
Ponder anew
What the Almighty can do,
Who with his love doth befriend thee.

Praise to the Lord, who doth nourish thy life
    and restore thee,
Fitting thee well for the tasks that are ever
    before thee,
Then to thy need
He like a mother does speed,
Spreading the wings of grace o'er thee.

Praise to the Lord, who when tempests their
    warfare are waging,
Who, when the elements madly around thee
    are raging,
Biddeth them cease,
Turneth their fury to peace,
Whirlwinds and waters assuaging.

Praise to the Lord, who, when darkness of sin
    is abounding,
Who, when the godless do triumph, all virtue
    confounding,

Sheddeth his light,
Chaseth the horrors of night,
Saints with his mercy surrounding.

Praise to the Lord, O let all that is in me
    adore him!
All that hath life and breath, come now with
    praises before him!
Let the Amen
Sound from His people again,
Gladly for all we adore Him.

Joachim Neander (1650-1680)
trans. Catherine Winkworth (1827-1878)

I trust you have enjoyed reading these true and accurate reports of what I have seen God do in my lifetime. My prayer is that the experiences which I have recorded will not just be a matter of passing interest to you. May they inspire you to reach out to know the presence, leading and supernatural power of the Holy Spirit, through the Lord Jesus Christ, in every area of your life so that you will be able to tell your children and their children how real God has been to you.

He is waiting to do all of this and much more as you give your life in service to him.

Samuel McKibben

Lightning Source UK Ltd.
Milton Keynes UK
UKOW06f0018110516

274009UK00001B/7/P